CW01560969

A New Life on Bali

by

Manolo Link

Translated by
Birgitt Sylvia Lederer

First published in English 2020
Copyright English edition © 2020 Manolo Link
ISBN 979-8699072477

Translation from German into English
by Birgitt Sylvia Lederer
www.birgittlederer.com

Cover design: Paula Nolan

All rights reserved. No part of this publication may be reproduced, distributed, or transmitted in any form or by any means, including photocopying, recording, or other electronic or mechanical methods, without the prior written permission of the author, except in the case of brief quotations embodied in critical reviews and certain other noncommercial uses permitted by copyright law.

This is a work of non-fiction. In some limited cases names of people and places have been changed to protect the privacy of others.

First published in the German language in 2009
The German National Library listed this publication
in the German National Bibliography.
For details see http://d-nb.info/1179716019

Copyright German edition
© 2018 Karina Verlag, Vienna
German ISBN 978-3-96111-706-2

German Copy Editors: Regina Karolyi, Monika Thees
www.monika-thees.de

For Gisela

with love

CONTENT

1 Goodbye

I no longer believed in coincidences, especially after all the inexplicable events I had experienced in the past few years. It therefore also came as no surprise that we did not fly over the Arabian Gulf, as had been the case with previous flights to Asia, and instead the flight path happened to be over Poland and Russia. Having said this, my hair suddenly stood on end, when minutes later I noticed on the flight monitor that we were flying over Leipzig. Gisela was born in Leipzig. It was where her life began.

Beside me sat my brother-in-law Franz, who had let me have the window seat, his head buried in his newspaper. After eleven hours we landed in Bangkok. This was the city where my first and last long-distance trip had taken me with Gisela several years earlier. Reminiscing about the wonderful time we had as we wholeheartedly gave in to our urge to travel made me miss my wife all the more. Five hours later and our flight to Bali took off. The tears welled up in my eyes at the thought of what lay ahead for us. I loved Bali, more than words could tell. Yet the reason for taking the plunge in immersing myself in this paradisiacal island kingdom for a third time, made me very sad all over again. When I caught sight of Bali beneath me, my emotions began to play havoc with me, much like the turbulence that shook through our aircraft as it made its way through the gigantic tropical clouds. In due course the captain gently touched down. The plane arrived amidst glorious sunshine.

I could not help worrying about the casket. The conventional way to send it would have been as a cargo item to be collected from the airport by the undertaker. I knew I now faced the very real risk of the cardboard box attracting unnecessary attention in customs.

"How are we going to get the casket out of the airport without the authorities asking us some unpleasant questions or worse still demanding that we open the box?" I asked Franz.

"Don't worry. Everything will be fine," he reassured me.

We still had to pay the mandatory visa fee and go through passport control. As we made a beeline for the luggage carousel I became increasingly anxious. *I just hope the casket survived both the flights intact.* After a short waiting period I noticed the cardboard box beside my small suitcase. Relieved I lifted it off the belt and handed it to Franz.

At luggage inspection I noticed a woman standing in front of her open suitcase. Even before I could hint to Franz that he should make his way to queue behind her because I assumed that not every passenger would be checked, an elderly official motioned my brother-in-law to him with an unmistakable hand gesture. Obviously he could not ignore the instruction. *I hope to goodness he doesn't ask what is inside the box.* Then the inevitable question: "What is inside it?" was put to Franz standing before the Balinese official.

"Ash," he replied self-consciously.

The official glanced back and forth incredulously, first at the box then at Franz.

"What is inside it?" the official ventured the same question again.

"Ash!"

I became increasingly anxious, while at the same time admiring Gisela's brother for answering the questions so candidly and in a seemingly calm manner.

"Open the box!" the official ordered Franz. My heart leapt up into my throat, I could feel the beads of perspiration forming on my forehead. Franz obeyed the order. A second grey cardboard box sealed and tied up with string emerged from the first.

"What is inside it?" asked the official increasingly impatiently.

He was repeating the same thing over and over again for what seemed like the thousandth time, I felt totally exasperated. Please let him go now at long last. Please, dear God help us and tell the person to stop being so persistent. The situation had become unbearable.

"My sister's ashes," replied Franz.

"Where does your sister live?"

"My sister died and the box contains her remains."

He fixed his gaze on Franz.

"Can you open the cardboard box?" was the next question that immediately followed. Franz pointed to the seal and gesticulating frantically explained that that would not be possible. An unexpected sense of respect had now somehow entered the equation and I detected a glint of uncertainty in the official's eyes. He had unwittingly reached an impasse, overwhelmed by indecision. With an impatient yet unambiguous gesture he finally sent Franz on his way. *We had made it!* My body suddenly felt lighter. I suddenly remembered what Gisela had said: "Take Franz with you to Bali, your command of the English language won't get you through the formalities." *I had to give it to her, she was absolutely right!*

As I consciously took in the sights on the drive to the hotel, people in their colourful sarongs and the distinctive green rice paddies, Bali immediately felt familiar to me once again. Our hotel was out of this world. Two porters were quickly at hand to help us unload our luggage. We respectfully declined their help since our suitcases were not heavy, something they evidently could not understand going by the expressions on their faces.

"Who's going to take the casket?" Franz asked.

"I'll take it," I ventured after brief hesitation.

No sooner had I stepped into my light and airy en suite overlooking the beautiful palm garden, I caught myself trying to remember which side of the bed had been Gisela's. A sudden heavy-heartedness overcame me with the realisation that I was holding her remains in my arms. She liked sleeping by the window so I placed the casket on the bedside table beside the balcony door. What wouldn't I give to be holding Gisela in my arms right now! To be able to share the excitement of the beautiful double room, the garden and the entire trip with her. It was often the small things in life that would have us thrilled to bits like children. Gisela had a way of showing her happiness openly and joyfully in a warm and affectionate manner. Her laugh was contagious, simply captivating, which was why everybody liked her. She was a wonderful woman.

My armpit was itching and standing in front of the bathroom mirror I tried to figure out what was causing the discomfort. At the hospice Gisela had asked me on several occasions if it was some kind of eczema. At the time I did not really take in what she had said. Anyway it now seems that she had been right. I stepped into the shower deep in thought. It was very tempting to go to bed straight afterwards. I was totally exhausted from the long flight and the time difference. However, experience from previous trips to Asia had taught me that the best thing to do on arrival was to adapt your body clock to the country's time zone right away. I got dressed, made my way through the lobby into the garden in all its tropical splendour and headed to the sea.

Deep in thought I ambled across the beach of Sanur. There was hardly anybody to be seen. A glance at my watch told me that it was time to return to the hotel. Back at the complex I relaxed in a chair, my tired eyes drifting across the ocean. Gisela had loved Bali and its friendly people so much. When she had set foot on the Indonesian island province for the first time many years ago accompanied by her parents, she was overcome with the feeling of finally having arrived. Bali seemed so familiar to her as though she had already lived there once before. She had derived so much enjoyment from this trip that her parents had made happen.

I looked up with a start. Franz had appeared seemingly out of nowhere and was standing before me.

"Hi Mano, did you fall asleep?"

"No, I couldn't help thinking about Gisela. Did you manage to reach Mr Sumastra?"

"Yes, he will meet us at the hotel at around ten tomorrow," Franz assured me sounding relieved.

We made our way down to the beach. The ocean was a striking deep blue. I felt the gentle breeze wafting through my hair. A Balinese woman came towards us smiling. "Apa khabar?" My question seemed to take her by surprise. "Baik, baik," was her shy reply, astonished that a 'long nose' as the European visitor is still sometimes referred to in this part of the world today, had addressed her in Indonesian. Next she ventured the customary questions in broken English. Where are you from? Married? How many children? Boys or girls? How old? The Balinese people find it difficult to get their heads around the idea that there are adults who are not married and who do not have children. We then said our farewells: "Selamat tinggal – May peace remain with you," I said. "Selamat jalan – May peace go with you," she replied. I immediately felt a sense of belonging once again. These people with their honest open smiles and devout hearts had the capacity to endow with love the hearts of those who had the good fortune of crossing their paths. Darkness set in quickly as is common in these latitudes. The silence around us was tangible. It had a soothing effect on me.

"What should we do tonight?" I asked Franz.

"There are going to be some Balinese dancers performing in the hotel garden and an Indonesian buffet is being served."

"I'd enjoy that. I'll go and get changed now then we can meet up in the garden afterwards."

"Okay, see you then."

Even though we got to the performance quite late, the waiter still showed us to a table close to the stage. It was set festively with a white tablecloth and matching serviettes. The moonlit sea had an eerie shine to it. There was not a cloud in the star covered sky.

The familiar sounds of the Gamelan orchestra rang out. The legong dancer was ushered in. It is a dance that has a special significance in Bali, according to age-old tradition the legong expresses the heavenly dance of godly nymphs. It is considered the most charming of all of Bali's traditional dances and every young girl here dreams of becoming a legong dancer.

Magical is the only word that will do justice to the young dancer who took centre stage in her brocade costume. She would glide down on to the floor ever so delicately only to raise herself up again in a seemingly transition-free move. Her fingers would circle around her wrists evenly while simultaneously coaxing her body into an arch with her outstretched elbows. How at the same time she was still able to concentrate on the movements of the fan, her footwork and eye movements was out of this world.

The friendly Balinese waiters made sure we had everything we needed. I watched the show in complete fascination. Deep-seated emotions began welling up inside of me and I could no longer hold back the tears that these brought to my eyes – the dance kept reminding me of Gisela. All I wanted to do was jump up from the table and make a run for it. I felt as if I were in a film. Nothing that was going on around me seemed to coincide with reality. In that moment in time Gisela felt unimaginably close to me. Thankfully the next dance was the last performance of the evening otherwise I would have had to leave.

I needed to be alone. I headed to the beach to give my tears free rein. I had a good cry. Then at some point I could not keep my eyes open any longer, wandered back to the hotel and got into bed. When I looked over at the cardboard box, it was the first time that I would feel a sense of love for the package that was all tied up. Somehow Gisela's remains gave me the feeling that she was with me. "Good night my love."

I woke up with a start in the middle of the night. Confused I looked around the dimly lit room. Where am I? What am I doing here? My body felt feverish, soaked through from perspiration. The vague remains of some heavy dreams were milling around inside my head. It was the cardboard box that brought me back to reality, calmed me down.

The shrill sound of the phone ringing tore me from a deep sleep. I looked at the clock. Eight o'clock! I grabbed hold of the receiver. A Balinese man on the other end wanted to sell me a daytrip. Still half asleep I declined his services. I glanced over at the cardboard box: "Good morning, Gisela." Although I would have given anything just to be able to carry on sleeping for a few days, I got up and went for a dip (that was what Gisela would say when she went for a shower). After donning a pair of light trousers and a short-sleeved shirt I headed to Franz's room and knocked on his door. A hearty breakfast was beckoning and we made our way to the restaurant in the hotel garden to enjoy it.

"Selamat pagi – A peaceful morning to you," was my greeting to the waiter He chuckled, slightly embarrassed at my Indonesian greeting. We chose a table with a sea view. The air felt crisp on my bare arms. We were served our coffees. The breakfast buffet itself reflected the warmth of the people. Pineapple chunks cut into stars, melon slices shaped into hearts. Everything was lovingly displayed. Gisela had been a great fan of pawpaw.

After breakfast we made ourselves comfortable in the hotel lounge to wait for the undertaker. The instant Mr Sumastra entered the hotel lobby I had a hunch that it had to be him even though I had never met him before. He had an imposing appearance in his reddish-brown sarong, a tall man in his mid-fifties who still had a good head of hair. From the very first moment, his soft brown eyes exuded a kindness that would touch my heart. I must admit though that I did wonder about his limp handshake when we first greeted. It was only much later that I would learn that in Bali a firm handshake was frowned upon because nobody here needed to assert their strength with muscle power.

We discussed the funeral ceremony proceedings with him and he informed us that we would be permitted to lay Gisela's ashes to rest at the waterfall in GitGit as per my late wife's wishes after all. In his last fax he had advised us that this would not be possible since in Bali it was customary to commit the ashes of the dead only to the ocean. Everything would take place in accordance with Gisela's wishes after all. As requested a Pedanda priest (a Hindu high priest) would officiate at the ceremony. According to the high priest's wisdom, one o'clock in the afternoon was the best time for the ceremony because the star constellations were at their most favourable then. With everything arranged Mr Sumastra bid us farewell leaving us with the assurance that someone would come and pick us up at the hotel at eleven the next morning.

Franz and I wanted to use the remaining hours of the day to do some sightseeing of the Bali that Gisela had come to love so much. It was the beautiful people themselves that she had held a special fondness for. She loved their colourful bright clothes, the respect with which they treated one another, not to mention their patience. She had a special affinity for the green masterfully laid out rice paddies, the palm trees, the orchards in bloom, the warm climate, the fragrances and of course Bali's religion.

Outside the hotel a number of taxi drivers were clamouring for our business: "Mister... transport? Mister... transport?" We quickly reached a deal with our driver on price and itinerary. His name was Rai and he turned out to be a quiet, level-headed operator. Our drive took us through Bali's capital Denpasar in a northerly direction where we got our first glimpse of traditional rice cultivation arduously carried out by Bali's hardworking people in the heat of the day. The intensive green landscape that was so distinctive of the country and had always fascinated me, lifted my mood somewhat. I too loved Bali. I felt a sudden sense of peace overcome me. I experienced a deep inexplicable sense of gratitude and love, even though it was extremely painful at the same time. It was as though something wanted to explain to me that there was a reason for everything and all I needed to do was to place my trust in the process.

Gazing out of the window I made a conscious effort to take in the lively hustle and bustle to the left and right of the road. People were bathing and doing their laundry in the rivers. An elderly woman was carrying a heavy jug on her head as generations before her had done thousands of years ago. The terraced rice fields were reminiscent of artworks in shades of green. It was as though I had been transported back in time to another era. Whenever Rai parked his vehicle, my eyes feasted on the small offerings with which the Balinese honour their gods, having lovingly decorated them with rice, biscuits and colourful petals. They could be seen everywhere. At the foot of sculptures of the gods, in the rice fields, by the front doors of houses, alongside the rivers and even inside the state-of-the-art airport building.

The Balinese people believe that the land on which they live and which they work is not theirs to own. It is merely on lease to them. This is why they treat it with great care, so as to be able to leave it to their descendants in a good fertile state. Exploiting the soil would be a serious transgression. It would anger the gods and the harvests would turn out lean. The Balinese people also feel that they form an intrinsic part of their country. They adorn it just as the countless butterflies, multi-coloured hibiscus blossoms, fiery poinsettias and brilliant bougainvilleas do. They lay out their rice terraces so as to please the gods. This is why they design them artistically leaving the observer with a lovely image in the mind's eye. Somehow everything on this island is in sync: the people, the animals, the plants, the land and the ocean all form one entity.

I became increasingly convinced that Gisela was trying to bring her Bali close to her brother and me and open our eyes to a country so beloved to her: "Look how beautiful and captivating it is here. This is where I wanted to be, I am here now and I intend to stay." Our stay began to feel like a valediction, an endless farewell stretching across many days and sacred stations.

I needed the Gents and asked Rai to stop the car at the next opportunity. "Kamar kecil," I said, he laughed. It literally means "small room". In only a few minutes he was already parking the car. While I was making my way up the stairs to the restaurant I felt a strange sensation overcome me. Then it became clear to me: I had been here once before with Gisela, Bärbel and Klaus. We had met the couple from the Bavarian district of Bad Tölz in the hotel on our last trip to Bali. Bärbel, a true globetrotter had convinced her fiancé, your typical Bavarian to get married in Bali. Bärbel had asked Gisela to be her matron of honour while I had been assigned the task of taking the wedding photos.

With nature's call taken care of I now had the urge to take another look around the restaurant. I immediately noticed the "Reserved" sign on the table we had sat at way back when, which was bizarre considering that the entire restaurant with its 60 or so tables was almost devoid of patrons. Even more bizarre was the chair that I noticed leaning up against a table. It was the only one in the restaurant positioned like this and the realisation that it was the one where Gisela had sat sent a shiver down my spine. I could remember the incident as clear as daylight. The chair had been in Gisela's way when she was trying to take a photo of us so she leaned it up against the table. I still have the photo to prove it. I descended the stairs deep in thought.

It was not long before we reached Besakih Temple, the mother temple of all Balinese temples. Franz was wearing shorts so had to arrange for a sarong which the lender draped around his hips masterfully. It is not permitted to enter the temple complex with bare legs. The psychedelic sarong matched Franz's white shirt like a charm. The sky was pristine blue and on this auspicious day we were to have a rare view of Mount Agung. Bali's highest volcano is more often than not hidden behind thick tropical clouds. The Balinese people believe that the gods have set up their throne in the mountains. To them Mount Agung is the navel of the world.

Slowly we climbed up the numerous stairs until the interior of the complex opened up before us flanked by plenty of praying believers in traditional yellow sarongs and white outer garments. An elder temple custodian came towards us smiling. Speaking good English he offered us his services as a guide. We gladly accepted his offer. There was much to be said for having a local who was in a position to induct us into the secrets of the mystical place. He took great pride in explaining the meaning and history of Bali's holiest site to us. Inside the temple area every principality of Bali has its own small house of God. The Besakih Temple symbolises the religious unity of Balinese Hinduism. With stars in his eyes the old man told us about a miracle that took place in February 1963 during the Eka Dasa Rudra – a very sacred celebration that takes place only every hundred years and is the biggest Balinese event of its kind. For centuries Mount Gunung had behaved. But as the preparations were taking place, Mount Agung started to show signs of erupting. The volcano erupted on 8th March during the sacrificial ceremony killing more than 100 people; destroying a lot of homes and almost the entire harvest. Given that, of all days, the spewing out of its lava mass coincided with the Eka Dasa Rudra celebration, the Balinese people believe that the gods were upset. Quite miraculously the temple complex was spared from the lava that was streaming down. Shortly before it reached the complex, for no apparent reason the lava separated into two streams now flowing to the right and left of the temple.

The 90-minute guided tour had us both in awe and we thanked our guide profusely. Still smiling, with a gentle handshake the old man bid us farewell and went on his way. It never ceased to amaze me how people could smile all the time. We made our way back to the sarong hirer who unravelled Franz out of his. A short detour to the "kamar kecil" and we were back on our way in the Toyota – our taxi could now pass for a sauna.

At Penelokan, a small mountain village, a unique view awaited us of the sacred Mount Batur – one of the world's most active volcanoes. Spread out before our feet embedded in a 15 kilometre crater was the dark blue Lake Batur. I was deeply moved by the landscape that Mother Nature had created at this spot. It was not long before we had attracted the attention of a few vendors. Even if these were a people who did not have much claim to material wealth, they possessed something far more valuable. Their faith, their love, their smiles, their work and the capacity to be happy was their very own claim to wealth. To me this ranked far higher than all the money and gold in the world. During my entire lifetime I had never met a people who exuded such a sense of satisfaction, were able to smile so much even though they had the war and violence of bygone days still hanging over them.

Rai now advised us to get going so as not to miss the spectacular sunset at Tanah Lot. Tanah Lot is a small temple. The name means land in the middle of the ocean and true to its name the temple perches on top of a rock mass located in the sea close to the shore. It is guarded by two massive holy snakes that live in one of the shrines. A brisk drive got us to one of Bali's main tourist highlights on time. The walk from the car park to the ocean would be one of memories past. I could not help thinking about the joyful anticipation with which Gisela had covered the same stretch with me not too long ago.

There were a few restaurants right by the beach. Seated, sipping an ice-cold beverage at one of these we took in a sunset whose beauty is unrivalled. Immediately after the sun went down most of the tourists headed to their cars or coaches but we stayed behind to admire the sky. It was a sky that was ablaze.

My relationship with Bali was becoming ever deeper. I was convinced it was the same for Gisela's brother. I already sensed that saying goodbye to Bali would be very hard for me. The night drive to Sanur through the sparsely lit streets had given me some time to go over the events of the day. Back at the hotel it was time to say our farewells to Rai, our driver, whom we had grown fond of. It was easy for me to grow fond of these people. I am pretty certain that their religion and the faith that comes with it can be credited for the more considerate and friendlier approach with which they interact with one another. The people here are more mindful and respectful of one another than in our European "elbow society" where some will think only of themselves. Obviously the Balinese people are not perfect; obviously they also have their problems that they are up against.

We found ourselves on the beach. The moon had risen above the ocean only moments earlier. An unfamiliar night sky bore testimony to all kinds of far away places. It was an exceptional night, clear and warm, its beauty intoxicating. Already on my first visit the island had had a tantalising effect on me – strange things seemed to happen here. I would later learn from other tourists that this too had been their experience of Bali. One German physician who had lived on the island for years reported light phenomena and mysterious events for which there was no explanation. He was one of those people who considered themselves to be very down to earth without any affinity for the supernatural.

We entered a restaurant not far from the sea. While I was eating my soup, the music sounding from the loudspeakers suddenly changed. I almost dropped my spoon. I felt my hair stand on end.

"This can't be!"

Franz looked at me baffled.

"The music – it's exactly the same music that followed Gisela and I around when we were in Bali. We loved it."

"Come on, it's just coincidence," was Franz's reaction.

"No Franz, I stopped believing in coincidences a long time ago. If I look back on my life with Gisela now, I can come up with a ridiculous number of so-called coincidences. It's like a wheel of fortune with the correct configurations coming up every time. As if someone had programmed it like that. All of this can hardly be coincidence."

Shrugging, Franz reached for his glass: "I must say that goes over my head completely."

I had come to a point in my life where little surprised me any longer. Things that were happening, and things that had happened, had no logical explanation. Obviously one could discount them with the word *coincidence*. However I found that difficult to do. I have often asked myself why of all the days Gisela had died exactly seven years to the day of our first meeting: 17th February. We were together for precisely seven years!

Before settling the restaurant bill Franz asked the waitress the title of the CD and the artist. "Degùng Sabilulungan by Suara Parahiangan," is what she wrote on piece of notepaper. I was determined to get myself a copy of the music.

Exhausted from the events of the day I was glad to be in bed at last. My thoughts went to the casket which stood on the dresser in silence, although it would seem to me that its content still wanted to share so much with me. I was certain that it held a multitude of secrets hidden inside it. Secrets which were not accessible to me yet, but which I was beginning to detect in the deepest recesses of my soul! I had a feeling that there was something infinite, incomprehensible and inaccessible that perhaps I would learn some day. Ash! What exactly is ash? Ashes to ashes, we turn back into ash. Ash in which infinitely more is present. Ash – I felt as though I had been catapulted into a world that I did not understand, but it was a world I did not fear. A world that hurt me but was oddly comforting at the same time. What I was experiencing were deep-seated feelings, feelings of love and of pain. Feelings that had forced their way into my world without warning, without checking with me, without asking me: May I inflict such a great sorrow on you? May I take your wife from you? May I push you into a deep dark pit? May I leave you feeling helpless? May I leave you to cry? May I do all these things to you? No, nobody bothered to ask me. Nobody had bothered to ask Gisela – she did not want this. She had often told me that she did not want to die, that she was too young to die. Nobody had asked her, but she had to leave. Leave her parents, her brother, her friends, me. She left and will never return to me again, she will never come back, never.

I secretly hoped that she would be reborn in Bali. I so wished this for her, that she would be born into this wonderful warm vibrant world. Reborn as a little girl with shining brown eyes and jet-black hair into a family that would lovingly nurture her, carrying her in the safety of their arms as was tradition here so that she would not come into contact with the ground for three months. The Balinese people protect their children as though they are small glittering stars that you cannot endow with enough love. This is why they thrive so beautifully and are able to pass on this love.

Love – Bali *is* love and will forever remain the epitome of love. This is why I so wanted to bring the woman I had loved so much back here. I had become greatly attached to the casket. The thought that I would have to relinquish it the next morning and would be saying goodbye to Gisela for the third and last time was unthinkable to me. If only I could take her home with me again. "Good night my love."

2 GitGit

After a restless night I finally got up at eight. I glanced across the room at the cardboard box and cherished it with all my heart. A refreshing shower helped revive my spirits somewhat.

"I feel really nervous," I confided in Franz on the way to breakfast.

"I know. How do you think I feel?" he replied with an unmistakably sad expression in his eyes.

"Good morning, coffee or tea?" a young Balinese waiter asked us smiling as we helped ourselves to the buffet. There was only one other man in the restaurant having his breakfast. Our table had a completely unobstructed view of the tranquil ocean enveloped in gleaming sunlight at this time of day. Sadly its tourist appeal eluded me on this morning. It was paradisiacal nonetheless. Perhaps I would come back here some day. I was surprised that I was actually able to eat something. After breakfast we headed to the beach.

My gaze soon lost itself in the surf, plunging into the frothy waves of worlds that I could not see yet feel. Fantastic vibrant worlds – worlds that I too would move into some day! I loved her. It was very clear to me in that moment in time. I loved her so much that I would gladly have dived into these worlds right away without a second thought. That was where Gisela was now.

On the way to the hotel lounge Franz looked at me concerned: "What's the matter with you, your eyes look weird?"

"Oh, nothing, I was lost in thought," I replied slightly dazed.

I had a sudden inspiration and asked Franz to take his penknife with him. We went to sit down at a table from which we could keep an eye on the hotel entrance. It was ten past eleven when a man in his forties entered the hotel evidently looking for someone. Franz got up and approached him asking him whether Mr Sumastra had sent him. He nodded saying he was a taxi driver. With that I picked up the casket and followed Franz and the man. An uneasy feeling overcame me as we walked to the car park. I asked Franz to double check with the driver. We got into the taxi and he drove off with us.

"Did Mr Sumastra send you?" Franz turned to the man, who instead of answering asked him where we were going. This was the cue we had unintentionally been waiting for and Franz told him in no uncertain terms to stop the vehicle. We climbed out of the car and walked back to the hotel. 11:20, 11:30, 11:35... I could not stop looking at my watch every few minutes. Impatience began to fuel my anxiety. After all it was the Pedanda priest who had proposed one o'clock as the best time for the ceremony.

Franz proceeded to the public phone to try to make contact with Mr Sumastra. It turned out that he was already on his way according to his son whom

Franz managed to speak to. It was almost noon by the time Mr Sumastra clad in ceremonial attire entered the hotel lobby. He apologised profusely and told us that our high priest had been called away to officiate at an urgent religious matter that had been impossible for him to postpone. Mr Sumastra explained that in keeping with protocol in situations like this he had not been permitted to ask the high priest's family any questions about the delay.

A dark red jeep was waiting in the hotel car park. Sitting beside the driver was the Pedanda high priest: a reserved man in his sixties with jet black hair, clad in a white outer garment. He greeted us with a slight nod of the head. The driver got out and opened the boot of the car for us. It revealed a flower arrangement of orchids. I placed the cardboard box containing the casket with the ashes beside them. I was certain that Gisela would have approved of the flowers. We got into the car and drove off. GitGit our destination was located ten kilometres south of Singaraja in North Bali. It would take us two hours to get there the driver told us. "We'll never make it there by one," I lamented but kept my thoughts to myself.

Alongside me on the back seat Franz was having an animated conversation in english of which I understood very little with Mr Sumastra. My command of english then was nothing like it is today and my brother-in-law turned to me every now and again translating snippets he thought were important. It seemed that the undertaker was inducting him into the mysteries of the Balinese faith. He spoke about death and rebirth. I listened more closely when he began explaining how the funeral ceremony would be conducted. He informed us that in Bali there existed only eleven sites from which its priests will extract water to be consecrated for use in holy ceremonies. I was glad about the fact that the water from GitGit was considered worthy of having this privilege accorded it. It meant that Gisela had inadvertently chosen a sacred site for her final farewell.

At some point in the course of the drive I suddenly began to have my doubts as to whether the waterfall in GitGit was in fact the right one. Five days before she died Gisela had first asked her brother, then me if we could lay her ashes to rest in Bali. I asked her where in Bali she had in mind. "At the waterfall we were at with Bärbel and Klaus," was her unequivocal answer. She was not able to remember its name, nor was I, although I was certain that it had to be in North Bali, I could still picture it and the surrounding area though. I have a photographic memory. If I see a face or place once it is committed to memory and I am able to recall it effortlessly. With names it is another story entirely, I tend to forget those quite easily.

When Mr Sumastra told us that it would be another ten or so kilometres to our destination it felt as though my nerves were going to get the better of me. I just hope that it is the right waterfall, I thought. When the driver pulled into the car park it felt as if a weight had been lifted off my shoulders. I recognised we were indeed in the right place.

Two hours had elapsed since we set out. It was very hot. I felt the sun burning my skin. A ten minute walk now lay ahead of us on the footpath down to the waterfall. I barely noticed my surroundings as we walked past the cacao plants, the multi-coloured flowers, the palm trees, the green tropical vegetation, unrivalled nature.

When we were nearly at the waterfall we passed small tourist shops. I glanced into the souvenir shop where in 1993 I had bought an unusual wooden sculpture. What had transpired at that same spot three years earlier now seemed like providence, a story that was destined to unfold the way that it did – or at least that is what I now believe. Many images began opening up before me in my mind's eye. I saw Gisela, Bärbel and Klaus sitting outside the souvenir shop. Gisela was so happy, her joy showed in her face. She radiated it. She was in Bali where she wanted to be.

While Gisela and the newly-weds chatted away I went to take a look in the shop. I was immediately drawn like magic to a particular woodcarving of an entrancing face that exuded beauty. It was as though in her features could be found the epitome of universal love capable of radiating out eternally – regardless of time and space. It did not take much haggling and she was mine. I showed her off to Gisela, Bärbel and Klaus. They all shared my enthusiasm. I decided there and then to name the woodcarving 'Cinta', which means 'love' in Indonesian.

As I walked down the path following Mr Sumastra who was carrying Gisela's ashes, I could hear Markus' words ringing in my ears. Markus is my son from my first marriage. It was a week after Gisela's passing and we were sitting at the coffee table in the lounge engrossed in a game of chess. Out of the blue Markus had blurted out: "You know Dad, she looks like Gisela". I followed his gaze to the woodcarving standing beside us on the table and felt the hair stand up on the back of my neck. I had previously though that the carving resembled Gisela, but had never said it to anyone. Now my ten-year old son was confirming this possibility for me. I have always been of the notion that children are very intuitive and uninhibited in saying what they believe to be true.

My sister-in-law Claudia reiterated this similarity a week or so later when we were sitting at the same table drinking coffee and speaking about our pain and about Gisela's death, trying to comfort one another. She was amazed to see it and I told her something I had never told anyone: "Ever since I put that carving on the table I've felt that she is holding some secret. Not only does she bear an uncanny resemblance to Gisela. I've been comparing pictures of Balinese women with photos of Gisela and noticed that her eyes and nose were features that actually resembled those of the Balinese women. Only the mouth region was different to theirs."

Claudia looked at me wide-eyed.

"And you know what else," I went on: "I've also learnt that the Balinese woodcarvers believe that when they create their artworks, they work a soul into them."

We both sat in silence. Claudia's eyes were brimming with tears. She and Gisela had been good friends. They had a lot in common. My sister-in-law's smile also had a tendency to touch people's hearts. I poured us another cup of coffee. We continued to sit in silence staring at the statuette.

Franz speaking to me startled me and pulled me away from my thoughts. I turned to him in a daze and came back down to earth and to the present. It was unbelievable what was happening to me – what had happened. It struck me there and then that there had to be in existence other worlds. I was overcome with the sensation of being out of balance, as though the earth beneath my feet was about to move. I shook my head vigorously and took a deep breath and asked Franz to repeat what he had said.

The high priest chose a shady spot slightly away from the waterfall. Turbulent water was no good for the soul of the departed he would explain to us later on. He carefully spread out a yellow prayer cloth on the ground beside a rock as tall as a man. An offering of fruit, incense sticks and colourful sweets were placed before the casket in the cardboard box which he positioned at the head of the display. The bouquet of flowers had found a home on top of the cardboard box. Mr Sumastra was crouched beside the priest lending him a hand with the preparations. The priest then got up, climbed up to a small temple nearby and remained there in prayer. We stayed behind and watched a few children play only metres from where we were. They had somehow managed to clamber down a huge boulder and were now curiously observing what was going on at the spot where they would usually come to swim.

Today a divine ambience hung over the spot. Colourful butterflies the size of my hand flew across the water, one even landed on my hand as if to console me. There were tourists swimming in the background, but their presence did not prove to be an intrusion. Balinese belief has it that the souls of the dead once freed from the body are ready to be reborn again a few months later. It was easy for me to adopt this belief. I said a silent prayer that her treasured Bali would become Gisela's place of re-birth.

Eventually the children lost interest in what was going on and went off for a swim in the water. I noticed how one of them remained behind. It was a good-looking young boy. He had already stood out earlier with his big compelling eyes. Gisela, look, the handsome one stayed behind for you, I though. Then he smiled at me. I found his presence strangely comforting and was glad that he had remained behind.

The high priest reappeared after a few minutes, removed some incense sticks from a cloth pouch, lit them and passed one to myself, one to Franz and one to Mr Sumastra. After lengthy silent prayer the high priest held the incense sticks above his head with folded hands and then stuck them into a bowl filled with sand standing in the middle of the prayer cloth. He then opened the grey cardboard box and revealed the casket containing the ashes – a brown earthenware urn decorated with floral ornaments. The priest was evidently having trouble opening the urn. He looked around and pointed to Franz's Swiss Army Knife which my brother-in-law had placed beside the prayer cloth. It was now clear to me why I had the intuition to bring along a knife. I handed the priest the knife and after some difficulty, he finally managed to open the urn. Next he ceremoniously leant over the flowing water and scooped some of the water up with his hand. He was very focused and solemn as he added this water, the elixir of life, to Gisela's ashes to prepare her for re-birth. Then he released some of the ashes into the river and motioned to Franz and me to follow suit. Franz released more of the ashes into the water before handing the urn to me. I took it from him, climbed down to the water and surrendered the remains of the ashes to the water which for me represented the eternal river of life. A prayerful calm overcame me. I could not help following the ashes with my eyes. Slowly they seemed to form themselves into a face on the water, it was as though Gisela was conveying her final greeting to me: "I have to go now, don't worry I'm going to be fine where I am going to." At that moment I had complete faith in what was happening and felt a tender love permeate my entire being. I looked up at the high priest who was motioning to me to commit the urn to the water as well. He then released the flowers and offerings into the water. A short distance away Mr Sumastra was quenching his thirst with an orange, that had originally been part of the offerings.

From a distance I saw a strange scenario unravelling before me. The youngster with the striking eyes had managed to salvage the urn from the water. Incredulous at what I was seeing I looked at the high priest for an answer willing him to do something. Strangely enough he was waving to the boy. The youngster hurried towards us, handed the urn to the priest. The priest held it in the water once more and in so doing deconsecrated it or so I assumed, he then handed it to the boy whose face lit up with sheer joy. I noticed Franz give away his penknife now worse for wear to one of the other kids and then release a small bundle tied up with string into the water. I was not to know what it contained and did not ask him about it again. I was not the inquisitive type and simply assumed that it was a silent pact between brother and sister in which I had no part. There was really no need for me to know anything about its contents.

Together we made our way up the short path to the temple where the high priest had prayed earlier. I took the time to take in the waterfall once more and I could feel my shoulders relax a little more. Gisela's last wish had been fulfilled. A spark of joy had sneaked into my being to circumvent my sorrow somewhat even if only for a fleeting moment. Everything had gone exactly as Gisela had envisaged and I could not have wished for the ceremony to have gone any better.

On the walk back to the car park the handsome youngster came to walk by my side. He seemed very content. The urn now served him as a drum. I was a little taken aback at first but then reminded myself that the high priest had deconsecrated it. Besides, given that the latter did not seem to have any objection to the strange use the urn had come to, I felt that what was going on could not be faulted.

I began to take a liking to the young boy who by then had told me his name was Putu and that he lived in GitGit with his family. He seemed to have no intention of budging from my side. We passed some folk who apparently knew him and they asked what it was he was drumming on. He proudly showed them the urn that had evidently become a new favourite toy.

I said goodbye to Putu at the car park and silently wished him well for his life. We climbed the stairs up to the restaurant and chose a table with an expansive view of Singaraja and the sea. The priest let Franz and I know via Mr Sumastra that he had found it to be a very beautiful funeral ceremony and that it had been a success in every respect. This led me to deduce that the targeted star constellation had still manifested itself in harmony with the proceedings even though we had been delayed. Yes, in retrospect I could not conceive of a more beautiful way to lay someone to rest. The only thing that did not suit me was that it had to be my wife.

We took our time over our late lunch then began to make our way back to the hotel. We drove in silence. The priest seated in the front passenger seat had nodded off. Every now and again his head would sink into his chest. Mr Sumastra, who seemed pleased with how the events of the day had played themselves out, looked at me every now and again with comforting eyes. I liked this man who exuded wisdom and gentleness. Whenever I would take a drive through Bali, I would use the opportunity to take in what my surroundings offered me. This time was no exception. These moments were crucial to kindling my fascination for this country. I was surprised when I looked up again and realised that our driver was already pulling into the hotel car park. I too must have dozed off.

We got out of the car, thanked the Pedanda priest and the driver with a gentle handshake. We then followed Mr Sumastra into the hotel. Franz paid the undertaker the agreed fee to cover the funeral costs and the transport. It was particularly hard for me to say goodbye to him, I felt as though I was saying goodbye to a life-long friend. He smiled at us one last time.

Once in my room the empty dresser played havoc with my mind. To escape the agonising sight I retired to my bathroom and got into the shower. This day would forever remain deeply imprinted inside of me. I went to lie down on the bed and stared out of the window. I lost myself in thought, thoughts about Bali, Gisela and a paradisiacal waterfall.

I awoke from my daydream with a start, someone was knocking at my hotel door. It was Franz. "Are you ready Mano? Did you forget?"

"No, I'm ready. Let's go."

"Suddenly everything feels much lighter," I said as I turned to my brother-in-law on the way to the garden. "Yes, it feels like that for me too," he looked at me with a smile on his lips. "Let's get something to eat. I'm so glad everything went so smoothly."

"Me too. Everything went exactly how Gisela had wanted it to," I replied.

In the garden the sounds of a gamelan orchestra greeted us. "Intoxicating," was what would come to mind. It was a superlative that had become my constant companion in Bali. On that particular evening hotel management was offering its guests an elaborate dance performance with a buffet. A waiter clad in white with a frangipani blossom in his hair showed us to a table not far from the band. I was fascinated by the faces of the musicians which exuded both strength and conviction. After dinner I felt the need to be alone and went to the ocean for a walk. The finality of having to leave Bali the next morning did not resonate with me at all. My only consolation was that I would be coming back here some day and went to my room.

The next day we spent what little time was left before our flight at the elephant cave of Goa Gajah near the artist town of Ubud, where we still went to see the ruins of the Yeh Pulu temple. I then managed to persuade Franz to agree to a detour into Denpasar afterwards. I felt compelled to look for that CD that had become somewhat of an obsession to me.

Once in Bali's capital, I immediately noticed that the drivers seemed calm despite the heavy traffic loads and nobody seemed to get worked up about anyone else on the road. I could not help wondering if it would still be the same if an accident were to happen. I had barely had the thought when a motorcyclist came crashing into the front passenger door. Both drivers stared at one another for a while neither seemingly prepared to budge. Strangely enough there was no attacking one another, nobody began ranting nor was there a barrage of words. Completely unharmed the motorcyclist casually got back on to his bike and carried on riding. Our driver did not even bother to inspect the damage to the car door and drove off commenting that it was nothing worth bothering about. I still could not believe what had just happened. I realised that I had inadvertently got the answer to my thoughts. This was really uncanny. I made a conscious decision there and then not to entertain any bad thoughts from thereon I told Franz what I had been thinking about seconds before the accident. All he could do was shake his head.

Curious, Franz and I inspected the damage once we got out the car on the parking level of the Matahari shopping centre. The passenger door had a nasty dent. This was hard to believe, back home there would have been a big scene. Not in Bali, here things are very different. After letting the damaged door distract me momentarily I now made it my mission to find the CD I was looking for. Even though I had promised myself to make a more concerted effort to allow life to take its course and not to question everything, I still could not help wondering how I had been guided directly to the correct shop display case inside this gigantic mall. The CD was staring me in the face as if it had been waiting for me. The shop assistant obligingly played it for me on his hi-fi system so that there would be no doubt in my mind whatsoever about it being the music that I was after.

Late that afternoon our plane took off making its way through the slightly cloudy sky, taking me away from a world that I had come to love so much and that had filled such a special place in my heart. I saw Bali slowly disappear beneath me. My only wish at that point in time was: Please let me come back here soon! I had a feeling it would not be all that long before I would return.

At the luggage carousel in Frankfurt Airport Franz and I both took the opportunity to phone our families. My parents were glad to have me back on German soil. They had felt uneasy about the whole Bali thing and the funeral ceremony there. Back in my own home which I had shared with Gisela, I was exhausted, but all I wanted to do was to listen to the cherished music right away. I took the woodcarving in my arms and for a long time just sat there gazing at this face replete with universal beauty. I wept but not bitterly. My tears were filled with love and warmth. Things were opening up inside of me for which I had no words. Feelings which were totally unfamiliar to me! I could see Bali in my mind's eye. I could feel Gisela's closeness. I lay down on the couch and fell asleep. When I opened my eyes again the clock on the wall revealed that two hours had gone by. An untold endless emptiness had permeated my entire being.

3 Seven years earlier

It had so turned out that on that particular Saturday I did not have to work for a change. I got dressed and made my way to the lift. My flat on the seventh floor of a residential complex was small but affordable. Outside it was drizzling. I bought fresh rolls, cheese and some candles from the nearby supermarket. For weeks now I had been having breakfast by candlelight with the notion that not only would it brighten my room, but also lifts my mood. Repeating the 'ritual' again this morning, I was suddenly feeling a little more upbeat and decided to take a drive to the town of Erftstadt-Liblar, a nice spot to go hiking and only some 25 kilometres from Cologne. With the washing up done, I grabbed my old hiking boots, made my way to the car and drove off.

Shortly before reaching my destination a strange sensation took hold of me, it felt as though I was going into slow motion. A newspaper! I was overcome by a sudden urgency to buy myself a newspaper. What with being on a tight budget I hadn't bought one in weeks, besides, it was always the same old news anyway. I had come to a fork in the road. The road on the left would have taken me straight to the designated hikers' car park, but instead I indicated right as though not of my own volition. Surprised at this action I drove my Audi straight to the shopping centre's car park, hurriedly made my way to the newspaper vendor, briefly greeted the shop attendant and grabbed a copy of the Cologne daily 'Kölner Express' only because it happened to be the least expensive newspaper. I was on my way to the pay point when the same sensation from earlier on where the road had forked, again took hold of me drawing me back to the newspaper racks. Glancing over them my gaze unexpectedly locked itself onto the popular Cologne publication 'Annonce', which publishes classifieds and personal ads. The focus I was sure would be on cars, radios, fridges, furniture and who knows whatever other random items were being bought and sold. Yet before I knew it my weird mood had me pick up a copy and make my way to the till, but not before hesitating momentarily because of how expensive it was. I walked back to the car, got in, placed the newspapers beside me on the passenger's seat and headed towards the hikers' car park, sneaking a glimpse at my purchases every now and again. I found myself giving my head a vigorous shake at short intervals to pay better attention to the traffic. After one really close call, almost jumping a red traffic light by mistake, I was relieved to get to the car park only minutes later. I stole one last glance at the newspapers, felt a tinge of guilt at having bought them, then pulled on my hiking boots and set off on the trail.

I had budgeted two hours. Hiking in the tranquillity of God's serene nature always did me the world of good. There was nothing that could better offset my stressful job and the deadline pressure that inextricably came with it. Nature would reenergise me give me answers to my many questions. At times I would even receive answers without having asked any questions. Hiking had a way of making my problems dwindle into oblivion, eliminated with each new step. Occasionally I would stop in my tracks, consciously take in my surroundings: trees, birds, a lake, rocks, beautiful things that were close to my heart. It would give me a strong sense of self-awareness, empathy for my fellow human being, all that was godly and that had created this marvel. A hint of joy was returning to my heart. The past few years, especially the past few months had been difficult ones. Life had been relegated to the tedium of work, honouring debts and alimony payments. How I was going to keep up with the instalments for my tiny flat often turned out to be a mystery. A phone had become a luxury that I did not even dare to contemplate. Unaffordable! I hadn't gone out for weeks, something that would no doubt have made a difference to my frame of mind. Fortunately I had ceased my beer drinking and smoking habits. There would not have been any money left for that anyway. For many years alcohol had been my constant companion predominantly on the weekend, but not a loyal one, always leading me into the abyss and the associated lows that would increasingly repulse me. A year had since elapsed. In the situation I find myself in now alcohol would probably have been my demise. I can hardly bring myself to look back on the many hours whiled away in smoky stuffy pubs, resorting to playing card games and knocking back one drink after another. Precisely as my grandfather had once done, then my father, both setting the example. It was commonplace, a pastime.

Suddenly my mind could not help drifting back to those newspapers. For some inexplicable reason the thought of them lying on the front passenger seat of my car gave me goosebumps. I had come across very few fellow hikers on this cold and wet day in January. I did not mind what the weather held in store, when I was out enjoying nature it brought with it a sense of well-being. As a child I already had difficulty being indoors. The dry air in the heated rooms did not agree with me aside from which I had developed an allergy to house dust. Your guess is as good as mine as to why.

Three hours later and I was back at my car with my hiking boots covered in dirt. I cleaned the shoes on the grass, placed them in the boot of the car and opened the driver's door. My hair stood on end once more when I saw the newspapers. I'm going looney tunes I thought to myself, got in, turned the ignition key, put the car in reverse gear and slowly edged my way out of the muddy car park back on to the road. I shook my head, couldn't help having a good laugh at myself and my feelings. The thought as to whether I was even remotely normal often crossed my mind. I knew that I was different from most of my fellow human beings. As a child I would set myself dares to convince myself and others that I was not as stupid as I was often told, or had come to believe. Anyway a large contingent of guardian angels was needed either to break my fall when I fell from trees. Or to rescue me alive from construction pits which I had inadvertently crashed into at full speed having miscalculated the tension wires with the height of me on my bicycle. I had broken my arm twice wanting to prove that I could jump further and higher than my friends. I had lost count of how often I had to have bandages or stitches after racing wildly. I had taken on the role of class clown at school. The other pupils liked me, especially the girls because I always made them laugh with my practical jokes and cheeky chatter. My teacher Ms Kloesel let me off the hook quite generously every time. She knew that I was only having fun amusing my fellow pupils without any harm intended. She enjoyed a good laugh. Obviously she had to tell me off. It was her job. She was a wonderful teacher, popular with everyone and we were all in seventh heaven. Then a male teacher by the name of Mr Engel took over. His name may have meant "angel" but to me he was no angel, and I often had a pain in my stomach just thinking of going into class with him.

I tried to remember what had been on my mind before the hike. No second-guessing that, it had to be my finances! Surprisingly a longer hike or walk had a way of getting my problems to dwindle and at times even disappear completely. Years later I learnt how God and the Universe support each one of us – but we have to be open to it! This was to be one of the most important insights I gained in my life. At the time I didn't understand this although I was aware of a new spark bringing hope into my dismal day. This glimmer of hope kept me going. Reflecting on it, now, I realise it was my love for my children, Ramona and Markus, and my parents that kept me going.

On my way back, in the town of Kierdorf some 15 kilometres from Cologne I popped into a bakery, something I would not often indulge in. Yet on this day a little more joyfulness and optimism seemed to permeate my day. I was looking forward to treating myself to a slice of my favourite baked cheese cake. In the end I bought two slices. Well-wrapped, they took their pride of place on top of the mysterious newspapers. I drove the rest of the way home grinning like the cat that got the cream, made my way up to my flat newspapers and cake slices in tow, closed the front door behind me and began to brew myself a pot of filter coffee. Having changed into something more comfortable I sat down on the couch, took a sip of coffee and delighted in the taste of the delicious cake.

I first paged through the sports pages of the daily I had bought. It was the winter break, there were no soccer games and the pages were dominated by winter sports headlines. When I turned the page, I was a little taken aback to see the *Lonely Hearts Column* staring back at me. I felt a barrage of emotions well up in me. If anything the personal ads were a stark reminder of my life. I pined for a woman in my life, a kiss, her closeness, her scent, sexuality… after all I was a young man! The chances of meeting a woman were not particularly good since I no longer frequented the kind of places where such encounters were most often likely to take place: in clubs, bars, at dances or other random events. Enthusiastically I read: "Friendly blond nurse, age 30, without any attachments. *Sounds good.* I liked the ad. *Highlight it!* Jutta, age 48, financially independent. *Too old for me.* Karin, age 24, student. *Too young.* Sporty brunette age 32 with a two-year-old son seeks man up to age 40 with high principles and strong character, financially well-placed and is fond of children. *Not my cup of tea. I like children but am not financially well placed at all.* Maria, 29 years young, blond, sporty and hobbies include: travel, tennis and reading. *Also sounds good.* Again I grabbed my highlighter.

After reading all the adverts in the column, I now picked up the classifieds and personals newspaper 'Annonce'. In the store earlier on I had already sought justification for buying such an expensive newspaper. Now it came to me as clear as daylight. My excitement knew no bounds as I anxiously scrambled to find the lonely hearts column: "Hey you! Are you also alone? Then why not meet up? My name is Gisela, I am 34 and I enjoy nature, squash, the movies, eating out and music. I am looking for a man around the same age as me who I can enjoy life's good things with. Only serious applicants need reply with a recent photo to Box Number KA-7962.

Nice and self-confident was my first thought. *Hey you!* It kind of tells me that she has a strong character. In a way these words struck a chord with me, barring the fact that we have the same interests to a tee and the age is also perfect. So this is what I replied:

Hey you, Gisela!

I am also single. We could join forces. My name is Franz-Josef, and I am 33. I too enjoy nature, squash, the movies, eating out and music (no, it's not a joke I really do have the same hobbies as you). I too am looking for someone to share my enjoyment of the good things in life. I would be delighted to have the opportunity to get to know you in person. I like to live near to nature, enjoy going for long walks, am a hopeless romantic. I am looking for a friendly, slim and unpretentious woman. You may call me old-fashioned, but I still believe in "love". If the letter and photo appeal to you I look forward to hearing from you and a photo of yourself. If not, please would you kindly return my photo! If nothing is to come of this I'd like to wish you all the best in finding a partner anyway.

Hope to hear from, till then warm regards

Franz-Josef

I enclosed a photo of my latest holiday in Berchtesgaden in the Bavarian Alps which a friendly hiker had taken of me on Watzmann Mountain and placed it in the envelope together with the letter. I took a stroll to the nearest post box to engage in the non-routine task of delivering my post and pushed the letter together with the two others I had prepared through the slot. Deep in thought I made my way back home happy to be back in my warm flat, switched on the small television set and stretched out on the couch.

At work in the next few days the personal ads that I had replied to were foremost in my mind. My colleagues whom I got on well with found my endeavour courageous and exciting but they also couldn't resist cracking a joke at my expense at every opportunity. It did not take long for me to receive the first rejection. In truth, it hardly came as a surprise. She wished me everything of the best for my future and I was grateful that at the very least she had taken the trouble to answer. Quite surprisingly the following day I received a letter from my favourite, the nurse, who was keen to get to meet up with me. In the evening I made my way to the closest phone booth like a nervous schoolboy on the first day of school, and phoned her. A friendly voice agreed to have dinner with me on the Saturday. The closer the weekend got, the more anxious I became. In the end we went out for dinner at the local Italian restaurant in Kerpen where I lived. I soon realised though that we were not meant for each us. On the drive home I was becoming increasingly despondent about ever getting to meet someone through a personal ad posted by a woman. On Monday I had had a gruelling day at work. I was on overtime duty and got back home late. I checked my letter box and could hardly contain myself when I saw the envelope with flawless handwriting inside it. I was already tearing it open in the lift. The photo of the dark-blonde woman immediately appealed to me.

Hello, Franz-Josef!

Thank you so much for your kind letter. I liked it especially because out of the replies I had received it was the only one not bursting with ego!

I like what you look like on your photo and if you aren't looking for a perfect woman, an angel with golden locks, I think we could become friends. What if we give it a go? If you like, call me!? (Any time until 10pm is fine by me).

Anyhow, that's it for today. I look forward to hearing from you.

Goodbye until then!

Gisela

After I had had a bite to eat, I made my way to the phone booth armed with plenty of coins and hoping against all odds that I would be in luck and once more the phone booth had not been wrecked. Nervous I grabbed hold of the handset and dialled Gisela's number. A soft pleasant voice greeted me:

"Gisela Gerhard!"

"Good evening, this is Franz-Josef."

"Hi Franz-Josef, it's so nice that you called."

"Hi Gisela, thanks so much for the letter and the photo you sent."

"It was my pleasure."

"I'd like to get to get to know you in person."

"Likewise! How about we meet at the Cologne Central Station?"

"No problem, perhaps on Friday at 8pm?"

"That's perfect, at the entrance by the flower vendor?"

"That will be great, I'm looking forward. Have a nice evening," I replied.

"I'm also looking forward and thank you for your call."

"It was my pleasure."

"Goodbye."

The next few days dragged on. My colleagues meanwhile had me on edge with their relentless jokes about my blind date that lay ahead. I could hardly wait for Friday to get here. In the morning I got to work early. It seemed to go on forever. Afterwards I dropped in at my dear grandma. It was where the family met week after week. That was how our grandmother kept the family together. I loved my family even though they too were not perfect. Besides, who are we to define "perfect"?

Of course everyone already knew what I was up to. At seven sharp I said my farewells and went on my way with my family's blessing and especially grandma's who said she would "cross fingers for me on both hands". Even though it was good seeing my family on a weekly basis, it was a relief to feel liberated from the torrent of words cascading all over me every time. The people of the Rhineland are known for their talkativeness, the downside is nobody ever bothers to sit back and listen properly. Quarrels in our family were a rarity and so much the better for me a Libra averse to conflict. Libras thrive on harmony, side-step fights and where they cannot try to find an amicable solution.

It was raining lightly. My emotions were heightened but in a good way. I parked my car not far from the Cologne Cathedral and made my way to the meeting point that could potentially steer my life into another direction. I kept glancing at my watch. I was early with time to spare. I am not fond of rushing. I have enough of that kind of pressure at work. The city all around me felt as though it was heaving a sigh of relief after the hectic hustle and bustle only hours earlier. Mirrored on the wet tar were the billboards dancing in all the colours of the rainbow. As long as I can remember I have always found big cities too noisy, too bright and too crowded. I prefer the quiet countryside, nature. As a child I was in my element when I could spend time on a farm. I thrived on roaming the forests with my friends, chasing across the fields behind the rabbits and being in touch with the soil and the smell that would always be reminiscent of the place I call home.

It was not long before I reached the train station. The massive wall clock read ten to eight to be precise. For a moment I got caught up in the chaos of the noise, hurrying people, smells and announcements. At the flower shop there was nobody to be seen fitting Gisela's description. I looked at the faces of the people rushing by. My heart was in my mouth. *It would have been so much easier had we thought of a sign to recognise one another: Red roses, a green hat, newspaper – No, actually come to think of it that's all a load of rubbish, I thought to myself. Let me try to remember what the ad said. Then I thought about the advertisement per se. Who on earth had dropped it in my lap?* When I scanned the area around the flower kiosk again I now noticed a blonde woman in a sporty trench coat. My heart missed a beat. It had to be her. Hesitant I approached her: "Excuse me, Miss. Um… are you Gisela?"

"Yes, it's nice to meet you Franz Josef," she said with a captivating smile.

"Likewise nice to meet you."

"I've hardly eaten all day, do you mind if we pop in at McDonalds to get a quick bite to eat?

"I know there's a McDonalds on the high street. Let's head there."

We left the station building, climbed the many stairs to the cathedral and put on our beanies. The pedestrian precinct in front of the cathedral was notorious for the wind howling through it. At McDonalds it was warm. While Gisela bought herself a burger I waited at the entrance. I was able to keep my hunger in check somewhat thanks to grandma's rolls spread with cheese and liver pâté that I snacked on before I left. Gisela came towards me mouth full and grinning at the same time. What a nice woman I thought, very approachable, pretty, nice figure, and I was sure she was intelligent as well. I liked her from the very first moment.

Strolling along chatting excitedly we made our way to the Schildergasse pedestrian precinct which was less crowded now. At the landmark inner city residential and commercial complex Bazar D'Cologne we found ourselves a small Italian restaurant to have dinner. Sharing our life stories over delicious tortellini and Pizza al Tonno, revealed that Gisela had separated from her husband six years earlier, did not have any children, was passionate about travel and aside from Australia, had seen all the world's continents. I likewise told her that I lived separated from my wife, had a son and a daughter and ever since childhood had dreamed of travelling the world to see as many countries as possible. I felt at ease in Gisela's presence. Our conversation flowed without any awkwardness, pleasantly; I would even go as far as saying familiar as though we had been friends for many years. Gisela worked as an executive assistant in a medium-sized company in Leverkusen and spoke English fluently, as well as Spanish and French. Unfortunately I could not impress her with any foreign language skills. I became painfully aware, then, that I should rather have paid better attention in English class at school than always amuse the class. My English teacher would send me to Mr Baum the school principal quite frequently and the punishment would always be lines from the English reader. Even so I liked our principal who despite everything was fair and had a sense of humour.

The time with Gisela simply flew by. The waiter came over to us apologetically to advise us that the restaurant was closing. We couldn't help looking back at him incomprehensibly the evening had gone by so fast. I accompanied Gisela to her car. Assuring one another we would be in touch soon, we said our goodbyes. I walked back to my car in high spirits and drove home. I liked Gisela, what or if anything would come of it, still hung in the air. One thing was certain to my mind. The evening could not have gone any better. When I got home I still lay awake in bed a long time before finally falling asleep.

I got up at five the next morning thinking about Gisela. After breakfast I drove to work. It was cold and wet outside. I would have given anything to go back to bed. I needed the work, without working overtime we would never get through the many orders. The company was doing well. It was thanks to the overtime worked that my finances held their ground. If the truth be told, I would not be able to survive without the extra hours worked. It goes without saying that my thoughts kept wandering off to Gisela at work. My colleagues were relentless about how the evening had gone, what she looked like, if we would see one another again. I told them how things had gone and that I was keen to see Gisela again. The day's work finally accomplished I drove home and fell straight into bed exhausted. It was an afternoon nap accompanied by disturbing dreams. As soon as I woke up again there was nothing more urgent on my mind than to phone Gisela. I walked down to the phone booth which thankfully still worked and dialled Gisela's number: "Gisela Gerhard" answered the now familiar voice that I had become fond of.

"Hi Gisela, this is Franz-Josef."

"Hi Franz-Josef, good of you to call! How are you?"

"I'm well thanks. I really enjoyed last night. I had a bit of a nap after work. I didn't get much shut-eye the night before. Um… have you already got plans for tonight?"

"No, not yet."

"How about you meet me at Cologne Central Station, the flower shop as always?" I asked hopeful.

"Yes, at eight as always?" Gisela laughed.

"That will be great, I'll see you later. I'm looking forward."

"I'm also looking forward. Bye for now."

"Goodbye."

I was at our regular meeting point shortly before eight. My joy at seeing Gisela again was mirrored in her eyes. As on the previous evening we eventually ended up at Bazar de Cologne and had dinner at the same Italian restaurant. With an excited glint in her eye Gisela told me about her trips to Bali, Thailand, Egypt and the United States. Her eyes would light up even more when she spoke about Bali, it was her favourite place. I hung on to her every word, fascinated. Ever since I had seen the Mediterranean beneath me from an aeroplane for the first time at the age of 15, wanderlust had become my constant companion. I was fond of Spain, the warming sun, its beaches, the language and the mentality of the people.

When I was in Gisela's presence time seemed to take on other dimensions. Once again we were the last diners. Again I accompanied Gisela to her sporty car. It was only much later that she owned up that she would not have minded being kissed on this evening. I had evidently been too caught up with her to read the signals.

"What are you doing tomorrow?" I asked hopeful that she would also agree to spend Sunday with me.

"I haven't got any plans yet."

"My kids will be with me and I would really like for you to join us."

"That sounds good. I'll be there early afternoon and bring along some cake."

"Perfect, I'm already looking forward."

"Me too! See you tomorrow."

"Bye."

I drove home in seventh heaven not able to remember when last I had looked forward to the next day so much. Somehow my life was gaining new meaning. The realisation had hit me that everything is far more fun in twos.

On Sunday morning I fetched Ramona and Markus in high spirits. At the playground I took advantage of my children's eagerness to play to prepare them for Gisela's visit. Shortly before 2 pm Gisela was at my door armed with cake and the most charming smile. Gisela and the children did not take long to become friends. While we were enjoying our coffee and cake, the doorbell rang unexpectedly. My parents were taking their Sunday afternoon stroll and thought they might pop in to see their grandchildren. They were pleasantly surprised at Gisela's presence. I suspect that is why they stayed longer than they usually did. When saying her farewells my mother gave me a telling look. Being the overtly friendly person she is, she already let on that she really liked Gisela. After Markus had showered grandma and granddad with kisses, he turned to Gisela: "Do you mind if I also give you a kiss?" Of course she did not mind.

While I drove the children back home Gisela waited at the flat. On my way back to the flat I suddenly had palpitations at the thought that I would be alone with Gisela in only a few minutes. I longed for a kiss, warmth and tenderness. Gisela was a stunning woman. Nervous I opened the door to the flat. Gisela was sitting on the couch smiling at me. I got myself a glass of water and sat down next to her. Markus' words were ringing in my eyes. In no time at all I was following his example:

"Do you mind if I also give you a kiss?"

"Not at all!"

At some point afterwards Gisela walked over to the window and stared into the night: "Shall I be rational and drive home or shall I be irrational and stay?"

"I won't think of it as irrational if you stay..."

4 I can call my happiness by name

Gisela would visit her parents every Friday. There was no way around it, at some point in time I would have to accompany her. After all she would want to introduce her new partner to her parents. The following Friday we nervously made the trip to Cologne. A warm reception awaited us and all in all it turned out to be a good evening with good food and no shortage of conversation.

On the following afternoon Gisela turned up at my flat unexpectedly. Her expression immediately told me that something was wrong. She was hardly inside before she burst into tears. I took her into my arms.

"What happened, why are you crying?"

"My parents reckon that since I happened to get as many as 17 replies to my ad I shouldn't settle for the first option, as they put it, and that I should check out some of the others as well."

I felt sorry for Gisela. She was very close to her parents.

"The important thing is how you and I feel about one another and that we make one another happy. Besides your parents haven't even got to know me properly yet."

I assumed that my old dented Audi, my worn out boots and my "poor people" jacket, as Gisela called my coat, did not inspire much confidence with her parents. Despite earning a good salary I was not well off. I could see her parents' point of view.

In time our relationship evolved. It matured slowly, not love at first sight, not *head over heels* in love. But it was a relationship characterised by slow and deliberate growth filled with tenderness, understanding and friendship. Not only did we become lovers, but also good friends. We could depend on one another and trust one another. One thing Gisela struggled with though was my name. *Franz-Josef* simply would not resonate with her. It absolutely took the cake when on one occasion she called me from the window with a "yoo-hoo" and not my name. I could fully relate to the fact that she did not like my name. I already disliked it as a child. My parents will have to forgive me for saying that. When my teacher addressed me as a *Franz-Josef* I felt alienated and not the one spoken to. My friends called me *Juppi*. Once I was all grown-up it got converted to the more adult *Jupp*, the people of Cologne seem to do this spontaneously for their friends. Yet *Jupp* would also not strike a cord with Gisela. One thing was certain I did not relish being called *Yoo-Hoo*.

"So what should I call you?" Gisela asked me grinning provocatively with her beautiful blue eyes.

While we laboured over a feasible name I told Gisela about a holiday spent at Waldfischbach on the Galgenberg Mountains in the Rhineland-Palatinate at the age of 14. It was with my best friends Jogi, Deddi and Manni. Bored on one evening in the 'Friends of Nature hut' where we were staying, we came up with the ingenious idea of inventing nicknames for us all. At around that time German television was broadcasting the popular series *High Chaparral* across the nation. There was one actor who always had a big grin on his face and who played the role of Manolito and like me he wore his hair slightly longer. My friends were convinced that I looked just like him.

"Mano!" Gisela burst out excitedly.

That was how my nickname came about. "My dear Mano," the words still echo through my being to this day. In time I got used to my new name. I liked it so much that I eventually began to identify with it. The next few weeks and months took on a distinct rhythm! Our lives could not be any happier or more harmonious. The working week was spent at Gisela's flat, the weekends we relaxed at my flat. Sundays were usually spent with my children. As before, on a Friday Gisela would visit her parents whom I had developed a good relationship with by now and I would visit my dear grandmother. It took us just over a year to come to the realisation that quite frankly one flat was all we needed between the two of us. I got rid of mine and moved in with Gisela.

A job became available in the company where Gisela had been working as a secretary for many years. It was as though the position was specifically intended for me and it did not take me long to make the decision to apply, and before I knew it they had employed me. A whole set of new challenges awaited me. I took a bit of strain leaving the printing house in Cologne. After all, my colleagues and I had become good friends and I had a great relationship with my superiors. I was thankful for what the many years there had taught me. One thing was certain I would not miss the dreaded daily commute to Cologne.

In October I celebrated my 34th birthday. I had never been so happy: I can call my happiness by name – Gisela. Ironically it is when time is at its best it wants to fly by. A wonderful year was coming to an end. The Christmas bank holidays were sunny with light snow and a rain recorded in Pfronten in the mountains. We experienced a sense of utter gratefulness that we were so happy. I thought what better way to crown our happiness than with a wedding and proposed to her in bed on a romantic evening. Gisela did not need to think about it, greeting my proposal with an unequivocal "yes". Gisela wanted her favourite cousin Ingrid, who lived in Munich to be her witness, so we decided to hold the wedding there with only close family and friends invited. Franz, Brigitte and Ingrid's husband would round off the guest list.

We looked forward to the event like kids in anticipation of Christmas. It did not take Gisela long to convince me of the wedding ring that had caught her eye. We had the following inscription engraved in the yellow white and rose gold rings: "Hey you! 17.2.1989" I placed the case containing the rings in my wedding suit that had already taken its pride of place in my wardrobe in readiness for the big day. Every evening before the wedding, snuggled up in our warm bed together, either Gisela or I would get up once more and fetch the rings so we could admire them. We had grown utterly attached and fond of them.

Our marriage was the picture of happiness. We travelled a lot and worked hard, treated ourselves to dining out at our favourite restaurants, took long walks in nature and every second weekend I would collect my children to spend it with us.

5 Why?

A few entries from Gisela's journal:

27th June 1994: Routine check-up in Cologne. The physician detects a lump in my right armpit. It is indicative of a swollen lymph node. He arranges for me to have an ultrasound on the Wednesday. It turns out, fortuitously I might add, that on the same day I acquire that pair of red shoes while shopping in Leverkusen.

29th June 1994: Ultrasound. Only the armpit shows up as somewhat swollen, nowhere else. A small consolation! I convince myself that it cannot be anything serious. By the same token, logic tells me otherwise. I drive back home afterwards, make myself a substantial breakfast and then leave for the office.

1st July 1994: I'm scheduled for another check-up on Monday after the weekend. That is why today I first find myself in Rainer's rooms (he has been a friend for many years and is now our house doctor) to get him to write me a doctors' authorisation note. I am afraid and burst into tears. Rainer comforts me, saying the sooner I have greater certainty the better. He is right.

4th July 1994: At the hospital. I'm the first patient of the day and hardly have to wait at all. Dr Grass says that I need surgery and that they will need to clear the entire armpit as a preventative. I feel sick to the stomach, I need to sit down. The vibrant dress that I bought together with a pair of red shoes on

Saturday may have looked great then, but today the outfit is doing nothing for me. It had been my intention to go in to work right afterwards instead I go to see Rainer to get a sick note. Once at home I cannot stop crying, Mano does his best to comfort me.

5th July 1994: We begin the day with a visit to the dentist to arrange for Mano's root canal treatment, afterwards go for breakfast at Jacobi, Cologne's iconic fashion house which boasts a lovely coffee shop. We order champagne but I struggle to hold back the tears. I'm so afraid. Having sat down and relaxed for a while I feel better. Somehow it turns out to be a lovely day. Mano is very loving and attentive.

End of the entries.

Again I think it is no coincidence that on the same day that Gisela went for her routine check-up, I stumbled across a title listed as recommended reading in a magazine in the dentist's rooms. Although I had already committed it to memory I went to borrow a pen from reception just in case. The visit to the dentist over, I immediately made a beeline for the closest bookstore to get my copy of: *We will meet again in my paradise* by Christel Zachert. Back home, I made myself comfortable on the couch and it wasn't many pages later that the book was already triggering some heightened emotions in me and I begun to cry violently. So many things were becoming crystal clear to me. It was a painful yet enlightening barrage of tears. I had not shed a tear for years, not even in times of sadness. It did not take me long to read the book from cover to cover. A sense of gratitude that this book had inadvertently been placed in my hands overcame me. Its pages filled with so much love was bound to help many people like me. Only in later years would the extent of what it had given me, taught me and had done for me in preparation, become apparent to me.

It was mid-July when I drove Gisela to be admitted to a clinic in Cologne. A few weeks earlier I had regrettably lost my job. The upside was that my time was now freed up for Gisela. Perhaps it had been divine providence intervening? Who knows? Sometimes something like that happens in our lives, the deeper meaning of which we only get to understand more fully much later. There was nothing more important to me in that moment in time than to be by her side.

The tedious admin out of the way, a nurse accompanied us to a room whose décor could not have been less inspiring even if someone had tried. White walls, not a picture on the wall, not to mention the small hideous plastic shower room. If you had been relegated to a room like this not really sick yet, merely the sight of it would guarantee to make you ill. It was incomprehensible how little was left to the imagination when it came to decorating hospital rooms. Especially if one considered that the *hospitalia* of Latin origin were places of sanctuary that in early Christian times extended hospitality and care to strangers, then it would make sense to give hospital interiors a more friendly appearance. Fortunately the other bed was occupied by a friendly elderly lady lending the whole scene a redeeming quality of sorts.

Gisela patiently went through the motions of the protracted routine pre-op examinations. The long waiting periods in between gave us a chance to talk a lot, all the time consciously trying to take our minds off the issue of the moment. My farewell from Gisela when she was finally admitted was tough. I would have given anything to stay with her the night. Without her the flat that evening felt cold and empty.

The following morning I drove straight to Gisela after breakfast. The Cologne city centre was unbearably hot, the exhaust fumes were irritating my nose so it was with a sense of relief that I finally sat down beside her bed and held her hand. At home I had felt infinitely worse. There I could do nothing for her. The course of the day saw her undergo more tests. I promised her with a heavy heart that I would be by her side when she came to from the surgery.

"The operation went well and your wife is doing fine," a nurse told me reassuringly in Gisela's empty room. I had a picture of Bali in my pocket that I now stuck on the wall so that Gisela could see it from where she lay in bed. I was convinced that the small embellishment to her room would make her feel better. I noticed that her neighbour had meanwhile been discharged.

It was with a start that I surfaced from the brief daydream the photo of Bali had me unwittingly drift into. In a daze I made my way towards the post-surgery recovery room. It took a while for a nurse to appear with a gurney carrying Gisela. She opened her eyes briefly. I accompanied her along the sterile passage. Back in the room I gazed at her face while she slept. I felt so sad for her. I could not hold back the tears any longer. My blurred vision caught sight of the photo on the wall. Palm trees, rice paddies, exotic flowers and a towering volcano carried my thoughts to Bali and a picture-perfect kaleidoscope world of colour.

6 My Bali

Gisela had been raving about Bali ever since our first encounter. "My Bali," is how she would refer to it lovingly with that hint of mystery in her voice that would never fail to put me in a reflective mood. She was relentless, had to show me *her island* at all costs. So it came as no surprise when on one unsuspecting day I came across a travel guide about Indonesia on our coffee table. It was not long before I too was in the grip of the fascination that this country that boasted the world's fifth-largest population, already held for Gisela. I soon found myself committing to an appointment with the travel agent at Gisela's side and without her having to exert any of her powers of persuasion at that.

The Bazaar de Cologne had become a place that held special significance for us ever since our first meal there together. We had come across a small travel agent within the complex specialising in long-distance travel. Over coffee, orange juice and a tray of sweets, it took its competent staff less than two hours to come up with the ultimate tailor-made trip for us. The itinerary with its own special set of dynamics hit the mark so much so that I even got to tick off an item on my wish list as well! We were going to Australia as well; it was only a two-hour flight from Bali.

It was at the beginning of September. Bursting with anticipation, we found ourselves ready for take-off on the runway at Frankfurt Airport in our Garuda Indonesia-operated Boeing 747. After short layovers in the Emirate of Sharjah in the Persian Gulf and in Singapore, we finally landed in the Indonesian capital Jakarta in the early morning. We had finally made it to our destination, regrettably our luggage had not. Baggage retrieval turned out to be a futile exercise, evidently our suitcases had already been sent on to Bali. They would be returned to us in Jakarta the next day.

It was on this occasion that we got to know Viktor and Monika, a physician and nurse from Bonn only a half-hour drive from Cologne on the motorway. They had apparently felt compelled to speak to us intrigued by how calm we had remained, even with our suitcases having gone astray. Jakarta was the first stop on the Indonesia trip for them too. We drove to our hotel together, agreed to give ourselves an hour to freshen up and relax a little. Then headed out to explore Jakarta where aromas from the markets that would remind me of Thailand and our first long-distance trip wafted into my nose. I could relate to these foreign fragrances, after all they opened up a world to me that I had already pined for as a child. Asia was beginning to become an ever-increasing source of fascination for me. The lively hustle and bustle on the streets of the Indonesian capital had me completely captivated. I was intrigued by the people's faces and could not help staring at them. The noise and exhaust fumes from the cars and motor bikes that flooded the streets were another story entirely, I could not get used to them.

A noticeably fatigued Viktor and Monika came to join us for breakfast at the hotel the next morning.

Viktor was the picture of exasperation. Not only had the feeble, decrepit and noisy fan failed in its mission to make for a more bearable night, adding insult to injury were the mosquitoes and miscellaneous insects that these two already sleep-deprived individuals neither knew nor wanted to get to know, dancing around the mosquito nets impervious to the heat and its occupants' wish to sleep.

After breakfast we were keen to explore our immediate surrounds and thought of hiring a taxi. As if 'knowingly' several drivers were already hanging around in front of our hotel, and ready to seize the day swarmed us with a: "Mister, transport? Mister, transport?"

"*Berapa harga?*" I asked a guy in his fifties how much he charged. This was followed by a torrent of Indonesian words. I had no clue what he was saying but luckily Viktor came to my rescue with his excellent command of the English language. A few minutes of bartering and we had a price and our destinations sorted.

Our driver who also proved to be a knowledgeable travel guide turned out to be an excellent choice. On his recommendation we first visited the Bogor Botanical Gardens. It was a two-hour drive but well rewarded with gigantic exotic trees, endless varieties of ferns, flowers, bamboos and grasses as yet unknown to us, transporting us into an enchanted grand new world. Perusing the gardens had taken us far longer than expected and even if it meant juggling our plans for the day a little, we could not turn down the restaurant on the summit of a pass that had inadvertently presented itself as the perfect lunch stop. The tea plantations that it overlooked seemed to go on forever and for the uninitiated like me their green hue seemed almost unnatural. The rice dishes the attentive waiters lavished on us were delicious. Strains of Indonesian music filled the room.

Gisela came across as a changed person. A transformation seemed to have taken place in her ever since we set foot in Indonesia. I could not quite put a finger on it. Somehow the aura she exuded had changed, I did not recognise it. She looked bewitchingly beautiful as if this country was coaxing her beauty to blossom into the utmost it could be. Just like a hibiscus blossom whose full beauty is only revealed with the first rays of sun.

After lunch there was very little time left for any further sight-seeing. Gradually it was beginning to feel as though we were adapting to the unhurried pace of the people and their country. The locals exuded the kind of patience and graciousness which even though strange to me was very welcome at the same time. They had time, nobody got upset about anything. Why would they anyway? Our European perception of what constitutes a problem is worlds apart from that of our Indonesian counterparts. Here people have a way of living with greater awareness. They also laugh more. Never forced, sometimes as innocent as the laughter of a child! I enjoyed laughing with them, reciprocated their unconstrained and forthright friendliness and was thankful that they had bestowed this gift on me. Stress was all that Germany's cities could incite in me, everything governed by a hurried pace that went hand in hand with a lack of time. Cities made me feel aggressive. In nature by contrast I was the epitome of calm.

Gradually I was able to see the 'picture' that Gisela had already tried to paint for me at home through her own eyes. Now I was beginning to realise why it had been impossible despite her best efforts. Words could not paint a picture of Indonesia, its people, the country, the colours, the smells, the joy and the faith. Only being there in person would allow us to imbibe it with our senses... more importantly with our hearts. Only when we open up our hearts can we see.

The calm in the car felt palpable to me on the drive back to Jakarta. Gisela sat beside me, we were holding hands. It was with heavy hearts that we said our farewells outside our hotel. Viktor and Monika had to continue on their trip. The next destination they were heading for was also on our itinerary, only for us it had been programmed in as ten days of relaxation at the end.

The next day we negotiated the heavy traffic to the harbour with the same driver from the previous day after having collected our suitcases from the airport. Ships, harbours and oceans had always been synonymous to far off-places and longing for me. The harbour precinct was massive, the mooring ground for an inordinate number of both old and modern ships. Scrawny men in threadbare trousers, upper bodies exposed and wearing flip-flops were carrying heavy sacks onto the ships across narrow planks. With the mercury already having climbed above 35 degrees in the shade it was a daunting back-breaking task. Gisela was less than impressed by the experience and decided that she had had enough of the unbearable heat and fish smells. We left the site and drove off to Block M, Jakarta's largest mall.

We landed up in a clothing store where I was apparently attracting considerable attention among a group of the petite shop attendants who were evidently amused by me. On the hunt for a pair of jeans, I soon realised I was facing an unexpected challenge. Although I classified myself as slim by Western standards and with a clear conscience at that, all the trousers that I tried on were too tight. The giggling of the staff, some covering their mouths with their hands in embarrassment, reached a climax when I asked for the *kamar pas* or fitting cubicle. They knew all too well that the clothing had been designed for much smaller and slimmer people.

The way in which our holiday was unfolding, despite the attention that had been paid to its planning, had me increasingly convinced that even today it should be standard for tours to Asia be categorised as "Adventure Holidays". Our trusted driver drove us to the busy airport early the next morning. Having checked in, it was easy to get carried away people watching. On reaching the gate the staff told us they had been paging us but obviously we had not heard it given the high noise levels in the airport. They explained that the flight time on our tickets did not coincide with Garuda Indonesia airline's scheduled times. Fortunately the airline was flexible and transferred us to a later flight and when the time came, a Garuda Indonesia staff member personally drove us out to the waiting plane. I was almost expecting him to take us by the hand given how seriously he was taking his brief to look after us. Our luggage that was now in a greater hurry than us to get to Bali had me worried. My remark that our suitcases will already have familiarised themselves with Bali's airport by the time we get there did not go down well with Gisela. She said she did not find my comment funny, still she laughed. By the late afternoon we were in the air admiring the huge tropical clouds from our window. Every so often we would catch a glimpse of a volcano tip. Indonesia happens to be home to 49 active volcanoes. Eventually Bali appeared beneath us. Gisela's eyes were glowing.

Our suitcases were waiting for us in a corner beside the baggage carrousel. The next leg of our trip was Australia and with check-in at five the next morning we decided to spend the night at the airport. After a light supper we tried to find a comfortable spot on the uncomfortable seats in the waiting room to spend the night. We were just about to settle down for the night when an unexpected solution to our sleeping arrangements would present itself in the form of an official who had come to inform us that he was about to lock up the airport building. We would have to leave and find somewhere to sleep outside the airport, but since it was too late for a hotel he had just the solution. Anyway it made no sense to get a hotel because of how early we had to be back.

So it turned out that I spent the evening sitting at a table outside the airport terminal chatting with Kees, a tall Dutchman on the road to fulfilling his childhood dream, while Gisela sitting beside me tried to sleep resting her head on her arms. If everything went according to his plan Kees will have cycled Australia, New Zealand and New Caledonia over nine months. He told me about his arduous preparations, how he had made notes in a journal that he was carrying with him on where to find vitally important sources of water in the Outback and what to do if bitten by a snake. At some point during the evening I somehow managed to get some sleep… seated.

Shortly before 5 am the airport was open. Just before 7 am our plane took off into the skies above Bali and the unique sight of a volcano peering between the glistening clouds made up for some of my lost sleep. As for Gisela, you could cut her enthusiasm for the fish cakes that the air hostess had served us for breakfast with a knife. Eventually Australia appeared beneath us. We could hardly contain our excitement at landing on the Red Continent, Gisela was even more in awe when she realised she could tick her final box. She had now been to all the continents of this earth. If someone had told me years earlier that I would get the opportunity to visit Australia one day I know I would have dismissed it as a pipe dream there and then, distant and unattainable.

Before they let us disembark two officials came to disinfect the interior of the plane with a spray in a plastic bottle to circumvent possible pathogens from spreading. Foodstuffs irrespective of what type are subject to strict import bans. Once in the airport building I could not help smiling to myself at the officials with their cream-coloured knee-high socks, shorts and cowboy hats. For a moment I thought I had been transported to an American Western film set.

We spent a wonderful nine days in Australia. What intrigued me the most, were the vast expanses, the Kakadu National Park with its Aboriginal rock art, the 23-million year-old Katherine Gorge and the Arnhem Land Region. The original inhabitants of Australia held a special fascination for me and I was convinced that they had a direct sacred connection to the godly. They believe in a world that had been imagined and came into being through a dream. To me this was a wonderful thought and I was firmly convinced that it must have been a beautiful dream.

Our days Down Under had come to an end. The time had come for nine unforgettable days imbued in Australia's splendid sunshine to make way for Bali now beckoning us with open arms. At the airport in Denpasar we booked an inexpensive hotel at Kuta Beach for two nights. At the restaurant that evening, boundless joy best describes the reaction elicited from Gisela when a Gamelan orchestra accompanied by Balinese dancers unexpectedly made their appearance during dinner. The gracious movements of the dancers had me completely captivated. Every now and again I would steal a glance across at Gisela who seemed to have melded with the music and the dancers. I could see her eyes shining in the dim light of the lanterns. Hidden in the music was something inexpressively enigmatic. Also hidden in Bali was something unspeakably mysterious. I saw before me Gisela and Bali and they were united as one. It was a connection that left me in a pensive mood.

Bali was the epitome of something as yet unknown to me. How to compartmentalise and organise these mystical torrents of emotion was still alien to my world of feelings. Even though I was open to experiencing new things, the sensations they were evoking in me tended to go straight to my stomach like being in love. You could safely say… butterflies. If the truth be told these emotions were making me a little scared also. I could honestly have listened to these strains until the end of my days. They transported me away, far away into another world. A world that felt right, holding me afloat with empathy, holding me in its strong and forthcoming arms. They gave me confidence which I would readily succumb to and I would gladly have held on to. But I could not reach out to them; they could only be divined with the senses. Strangely my heart and soul seemed to comprehend all of this. At that moment in time I felt a deep, intense love for Gisela who had placed her hand in mine smiling at me. Encapsulated in her eyes was everything that I felt, longed for as it were. The whole world was captured in the glorious azure blue hue.

A waitress asked whether she could offer us another drink. She had startled me, I stared back at her, shook my head, looked at Gisela then turned back to the dancers, at pains to understand what was going on inside me and let the Gamelan sounds take hold of me once more. *Bali – what are you doing to me?* Gisela no longer needed to go to great lengths to bring *her Bali* into my reach, to have me understand it. After tonight what she had always tried to convey had become as clear as daylight to me and I said a silent thank you. I was becoming increasingly conscious of how valuable our love was. I stroked her hair. Exhaustion had overcome me, overwhelmed by the events of the day. "Let's go to bed," said Gisela kissing me on the lips. I felt wide awake once again. The music had ended. As always we would fall asleep, holding hands. I awoke during the night, stared at the ceiling wide awake only to discover two geckos chasing some mosquitoes. Geckos are supposed to bring good luck. It took me a while to get used to them. Gisela was in a deep uninterrupted sleep. I could not help thinking back on the previous night which was already beginning to feel unreal by now.

The shiny backs of tourists enjoying a massage in the blazing sun greeted us on the beach the next day, as did young men touting watches and souvenirs while children played in the warm water. We found ourselves in the midst of a kaleidoscope world of colour after a hearty breakfast at our hotel. Our beach walk took us past hotels that resembled small tropical paradises, their buildings reaching no higher than the palm trees as required by law. The complexes were carefully tended to daily by staff clad in colourful sarongs, a frangipani blossom decorating their hair, a broom made of straw to complete the picture. "Tell me, darling, do we really have to leave here again?" I asked Gisela. "We still have plenty of days to enjoy it all. For now just don't think about having to leave it all behind," was her reply. Gisela had often told me that she would rather live in Bali than elsewhere in the world.

On another morning we were headed on a bus to Bali's Padang Bai Harbour. Already en route we regretted having planned spending ten days on Lombok Island. Now we had no choice, a hotel room had been reserved for us and we had already paid for it in advance. I managed to have a small mishap during the wait at the harbour, breaking a tooth opening a water bottle. It was an incident that would leave me gap-toothed for the rest of my trip. I probably looked hilarious. I then had the ingenious idea of doing as the locals do and from then on every time I laughed held my hand in front of my mouth. It had Gisela in stitches.

The ferry took off at 2 pm. Gisela would much rather have flown. On closer observation of the ferry that had evidently seen better days it was a no-brainer when it came to deciding on the mode of transport for our return journey. Due to the rough seas the crossing of the 30 kilometre-wide and 3000 metre deep Lombok Strait was anything but a pleasant experience.

We had made it to Lembar Harbour on Lombok's west coast just as the sun was setting. All around us there were fishing boats gliding towards the shore without a sound. The PA system of the ferry sounded flute music that came towards us in bizarre windswept tones. The smoke of exotic cigarettes was wafting around my nose. It was a sweet smell that only served to heighten the intensity of all that was going on around me.

The ferry finally docked. It was a relief to be on terra firma once again. A grey driverless minibus with the name of our hotel stuck to the inside of the windscreen was waiting in the parking lot. No sooner had we reached the car, did the driver with his long black hair appear out of nowhere. It was getting dark quickly and he managed to get us to the hotel through the unlit streets in one piece in no time. We checked in to the Senggigi Beach Hotel, ordered a sandwich and then fell into the big comfortable bed.

Our days in Lombok were taken up with swimming, beach walks, day trips, reading and sheer relaxation. Towering over us throughout that time at 3726 metres above sea level was Indonesia's second-highest volcano, Mount Rinjani. The predominantly Islamic population in the fertile south of the island cultivates coffee and rice. Tourists consider Lombok a cost-effective alternative to Bali. Admittedly, when it comes to its beauty Lombok with its population of nearly two-and-a-half million people certainly does not have to worry about being overshadowed by its sister island Bali! Even so, we could not help the partiality we felt towards Bali. At the end of the day Lombok lacked that je ne sais quoi that Bali manifested so effortlessly.

Ten days in Lombok were more than enough. We were not sad to leave the island behind us and keen to get the flight on the small propeller plane over and done with. It was not often that I would get into the window seat of an aircraft and have to use my technical skills to improvise and prevent a stray wall panel from coming unstuck even further from the thin cables to which it had been precariously fastened.

The fact that the flight assistant then made himself comfortable on an old wooden box ready for take-off did very little to appease my growing uneasiness any further. The door to the cockpit was open and we could watch the captain and his co-pilot prepare for take-off. Gisela and I made light of the goings-on before us with a little banter to take off the edge. The remaining passengers sat stoned-faced evidently unable to see a redeeming quality in what to us had become our own little adventure. Given the short flight distance, it was not necessary for the craft to fly very high. With the view of the ocean and Bali the focal point in the foreground, it felt as though the pilot had rewarded our patience in the face of the plane's shortcomings with this postcard perfect view. The landing turned out to be another adventure in itself and I could not help pulling up my feet towards me and taking on the brace position when the aircraft approached the runway, not far from the water's edge and swaying slightly. When I got out of my seat, lo and behold, the wall panel came towards me once again. I could not help laughing but this time left it hanging.

We were back in Bali. Sadly we had to continue straight on to the next leg as our flights home had already been booked. After a five-hour delay we reluctantly boarded the jumbo jet, no lose wall panels this time round and embarked on our return journey to Frankfurt with layovers in Jakarta, Singapore and Abu Dhabi. Thirty-seven hours after setting off from Lombok we finally reached our destination. A unique and unforgettable trip had finally come to an end.

7 Living with hopes and fears

Dr Grass, who had performed the surgery on Gisela, entered the room jolting me back to reality. He shook my hand, looked at me pensively and said: "The operation went well. As a precaution we had to remove all the lymph nodes. Once the histological findings become available in a few days time we will have greater certainty and I can be more specific." I felt sick to the stomach. Dr Grass bent over Gisela who was still sleeping and checked the colour of the lymphatic fluid being carried by a tube to a bottle standing on the floor next to the bed. "If your wife needs anything please ring for the nurse," he added and disappeared through the door.

I sank down into a chair, wanted to shout from the rooftops, the pain I felt was so unbearable. Gisela did not deserve that. I found myself negotiating with God: "Why her? Such a wonderful person! Please look after her and let her get well again." I felt my heart cramp up from suffering. Gisela opened her eyes, looked at me and smiled. I kissed her dry lips, stroked her face and started to cry. She was not allowed to drink anything yet so at regular intervals I moistened her lips with a wad of cotton wool dipped in water. She threw up a number of times.

Everyone liked Gisela. Everyone entering her room would be gifted with a smile. The nurses looked after her caringly, delivered their best, always lent a listening ear and helped wherever they could. I was starkly aware of how comparatively small their remuneration was in comparison to how hard they worked and the knowledge base they prided themselves in. As far as I was concerned double the earnings would have been befitting.

After a week of uncertainty that simply would not come to an end, the prognosis became available. Of the 27 lymph nodes removed, 20 had been cancerous. Things could not have been worse. We were utterly shocked and Dr Grass's statistical analysis did little to appease our fears and only served to rub salt into the wound: "With a clinical picture like this there is 50 percent likelihood that further organs will be attacked by the cancer cells in the next few years." I could not comprehend his utterances. How on earth can you further burden a patient in the situation Gisela found herself with such hopeless words? I would have thought that counselling on commencing the healing process would have been far more appropriate and beneficial. After Dr Grass had left the room, I took Gisela in my arms and assured her that we would focus on wellness not on illness and that I would do everything humanly possible to help her.

Numerous visits from her parents, brothers and friends literally gave Gisela a new lease of life. The many phone calls and letters she received moved me as much as they did her. If anything, a time like this was proof of the value true friends held. As for the conversations with the doctors treating Gisela, I found them to be anything but helpful. At best, evasiveness was the order of the day when I dared broach the idea of alternative curative treatments, at worst outright dismissal. Even if it may now seem that I had lost all confidence in the doctors during those days, it was not entirely the case although something told me that they had already given up on her. That is what bothered me the most.

They had given Gisela six months to live.

It freaked me out and more so that she had been told. It was mind-boggling to me that one individual could presume to have it in his power to tell a fellow human being how much time she still had to live. Worse still, how was it even possible for the conscience to inflict such a shock utterance that would irreparably burden the immune system of the patient? If my physician does not believe in my recovery, then who will? I had read of people taking their lives after a diagnosis like this. By contrast I had also read that there were those who were still able to enjoy many living years, refusing to succumb to medical prognoses.

I am firmly of the conviction that the belief in recovery will go a long way in conquering illness. The more people who believe in it, the more likely recovery will prevail. By the same token, resign yourself to not making it and the chances are you will not make it! Self-love and a love for life is the key!

In the days that followed I was fast becoming a walking encyclopaedia on cancer and its cures. I learnt that each had its own set of dynamics and along with it, its own treatment paths. Every new insight had me wavering between hope and doubt. If anything, being able to conceptualise the cancer was giving me a sense of control, the illusion of not feeling so helpless. Gisela and I spoke about her condition often. We also spoke about death even if it scared us. Were we to sidestep such an important topic that affected us both, it would have scared us even more. We saw death not as an end in itself, but an opportunity for people to live on for eternity.

Since all the lymph nodes had to be removed Gisela had to remain vigilant of the risks of carrying heavy weights, ironing, using the oven, using knives etc. A sonography had to be done and with it there came one small glimmer of hope. The rest of Gisela's body showed no sign of any metastases. Moreover, she was gradually beginning to feel better from one day to the next. We managed to break the routine of daily life at the clinic with short walks in the area and every so often would treat ourselves to a good meal at an Italian restaurant close by. We were ecstatic when we eventually learnt that Gisela was to be discharged. Our lovely neighbour, Daniel, who was fast on the road to becoming a top-notch doctor and his exquisite partner, Sandra, a nurse, both of whom had been an invaluable crutch all this time, had left this note on our front door:

If every glimmer of hope can be likened to a good deed —
— Then, enthusiasm is definitely what we need!

For infinitely more powerful is the faith of one person
than the feigned concern 99 people might let on −
− With it we are able to be strong and conquer the world!
Dear friend, having you back is indeed unequalled!
WELCOME HOME GISELA!

Gisela burst into tears, but they were tears of joy. I had covered the couch with some of the cuddly toys that we had gifted one another with on occasion as my welcome home gesture. The weeks that followed saw Gisela go for regular lymph drainage sessions, we went for walks, Gisela focussed on good nutrition and she went to visit her parents and friends often. We conversed a lot, very openly. She was doing well. "Now more than ever," was her motto. In August, on the recommendation of the doctors she headed for follow-up reconvalescence treatment at a Medical Wellness Resort at a clinic in Freiburg in southern Germany… hopeful!

A few entries from Gisela's journal:

Tuesday, 23rd August 1994: Arrival at the Medical Wellness Resort in Freiburg for the follow-up reconvalescence treatment. The train pulled into the station a few minutes late on my departure. I have lunch in the dining car and after registering at the clinic a hot snack is served at around 2:30 pm. My room is light and friendly, unfortunately it overlooks the car park and the street. In the afternoon when my suitcases arrive I go about the task of unpacking them. Then Dr Boden comes to introduce himself and later Ms Wolter, the nurse who had been the first point of contact on my arrival comes by. At 5:30 pm she takes me on a tour of the clinic to show me everything. Afterwards it is time for supper. I share a table with three nice elderly women who welcome me warmly. The buffet is substantial and well-balanced. Just after eight I call Mano to tell him how my day went. He is relieved to hear that the place and its people are so congenial because that morning before it was time to leave I had been very sad. I feel much better after the phone call. Let's see what the morning has in store. Can you believe it, now my arm is also aching!

Wednesday, 24th August, Medical Wellness Resort Day 1: After breakfast a young doctor comes by to take blood. At 11:30 am it is the doctors' rounds. Dr Mandell, the senior physician, advises me to wear my ring on my left hand because the right hand is susceptible to swelling. German tradition has it that the wedding band is worn on the right hand. He is very much in favour of the mistletoe therapy, an alternative would be Echinacea. The latter has the advantage that it can be taken orally as opposed to having to inject oneself as in the case of the mistletoe. He says both preparations are the same in terms of their effect and side-effects. They strengthen the immune system and both are long-term therapies (two to five years). We discuss what I can expect from the treatments here and he reckons that together we will be able to achieve positive outcomes like restoring mobility to my right arm, regaining fitness, losing weight and the benefits of psychological care. I would also be issued with a disability pass. In the admission examination Dr Boden had recommended that Echinacea be prescribed. They will do another blood test for that in the morning so that I will be able to start taking the tincture. At present there is a study being conducted at Freiburg University on taking this preparation, so that its benefits can be substantiated. As from tomorrow I will be on a 1500 calorie diet, am booked for fitness training sessions, lymph drainage and swimming.

Thursday, 25th August, Medical Wellness Resort Day 2: After the blood test I go into town to do some shopping. At 11:20 am I am back with the intention of going to see Mr Bender the psychologist, but I need to put my arm up first it is so swollen. At 1 pm I go for my lymph drainage. The young male masseuse gives me an in-depth explanation of the lymphatic system and its role. I have to be very careful because my arm is at risk. I must avoid injuring myself (not cut my finger), exerting myself (carry heavy bags or play badminton) and avoid heat (like the sauna, hot baths, the sunbed). He then measures the circumference of both arms to draw a comparison. After supper I join a walk organised by Ms Rufer.

Friday, 26th August, Medical Wellness Resort Day 3: Fitness training at 9 am. It is utterly exhausting. Jogging and stretching do not agree with me at the moment, but then again there is no way I could have expected it to be any different. It has only been eight weeks since the operation. I am meanwhile also taking 30 Echinacea drops three times daily for five days, after which I will be taking a three-day break from them. They taste dreadful but I manage to get them down with water which is permissible.

Saturday, 27th August, Medical Wellness Resort Day 4: We go into town in the morning, walk for about three hours and my arm is doing very well. The only thing is that my muscles are aching from the fitness training. We buy postcards, stamps and shoes. We take the train back because it is getting late and we did not realise we had been dawdling. It is a great afternoon. Ms Wolfermann is a lovely person. In the evening I take the postcards to the postbox and go to bed early.

Sunday, 28th August, Medical Wellness Resort Day 5: This afternoon I go on an excursion with Ms Wolfermann to the Schluchsee, a lake in the Black Forest. Her train ticket is valid for an extra person accompanying her, so I don't need one. I spend the morning prior to our outing writing letters and cards and when I write to Irmgard, I cannot help crying. In my mind's eye I can hear 'Kiseo Sobet' the Swahili song which means a "wonderful world" and which she loves so much. The hike that afternoon turns out to be brilliant. We choose the path along the shore of the lake. Then enjoy a picnic of grapes and peaches on a large sun-kissed rock. By 8 pm I am ready to have supper. A young nurse still comes by to introduce herself, Mano also calls and later on I phone Mum. I sleep exceptionally well. Then again I am tired, after all it has been a very busy day.

Monday, 29th August, Medical Wellness Resort Day 6: At 9 am I am off to fitness training. It is being held in the shade on the lawn outdoors with jogging and other exercises. It is followed by autogenic training. Everything goes well. Dr Wolter who is responsible for me subsequently has a chat with me. He approves the extension of the programme and will take care of it. He adds water aerobics to my exercise regimen, saying that because I am strong in fitness training, the chair exercises & limited mobility fitness gymnastics are too sluggish for me. In the afternoon I attend a lecture on the role of the immune system with the manifestation of tumours. I learn that there are many preventative paths, but because they have not been around that long they are just beginning to come into their own. The swimming session in the evening is great fun.

Tuesday, 30th August, Medical Wellness Resort Day 7: I have a lymph drainage session at noon. I find it very agreeable. The discussion group in the afternoon is not very helpful; even so I'll go again. The water ballet is much too short, I really enjoy it. In the evening I join Ms Wolfermann and attend the slide show on wild flowers and herbs. I feel exhausted and all I can think of is turning in for the night.

Wednesday, 31st August, Medical Wellness Resort Day 8: The fitness training session in the morning gets me working up a sweat. I absolutely must get fitter. There are a lot of arm exercises and I keep up as best as I can. Afterwards it is time for the head physician's visit. Dr Bartel asks me if I have any concerns. I assure him I have none. Since they only received my documentation yesterday they are still deciding on a possible treatment for me. He says we will still discuss it. The fitness training ends up being more of a chat session than a workout. I'm sure Ms Keller is also a qualified psychologist and knows what she is doing. I buy myself a 'Regio-Ticket' so I can use the trains in the area whenever I want to and I register for the evening walk the next day. I've got mail! Christel in Berlin has written me a letter. I must get her address from Mano. We are invited to attend a storytelling evening.

Thursday, 1ˢᵗ September, Medical Wellness Resort Day 9: I've been in a great mood all day. To start the day the scale had dropped all of three pounds. After water ballet I still have a quick two-minute chat with Ms Keller. The lymph drainage feels good. At physio with Ms Keller my arm is doing so well that she asks me what other work she can do with me. In the end we simply end up philosophising (don't know why I choose to use such a frightfully highfalutin word) about life. The discussion group after lunch is very interesting. It centres on the focal theme: "Why did I get cancer?" Actually all illness goes back to a weakened psyche. Each and every one of us will have experienced some or other event beforehand, be it on a personal or professional level, that would become decisive in the disease manifesting itself. Even so, this is not a question that can be answered without ambiguities. Later in the day I receive a letter from Mano. He tells me he is listening to 'Kiseo Sobet' that he misses me and can't wait to see me. I look for my tape recording of the song and listen to it on my walkman, all the time dancing around my room ecstatically and re-reading the letter. Mano is coming to visit, I couldn't be happier. I go for a walk with the group. We stop for a bite to eat and I end up eating half of Ms Kühn's pancake as well. Mano phones me that evening. Before I turn in for the night Ms Wolfermann brings me a pot of herbal tea to my bedside. She is very sweet. Tomorrow I will write Mano a letter.

Friday, 2ⁿᵈ September, Medical Wellness Resort Day 10: Today I put my name down for the outing to Lake Titisee. I wonder how that will turn out. In the afternoon I go into town with Ms Wolfermann. I spoil myself and buy myself some nail polish. After my swim in the evening I still spend an hour on the phone. I also go and post the letter to Mano but the post box had already been emptied which means he will only get my letter on Monday.

Saturday, 3rd September, Medical Wellness Resort Day 11: Before lunch I go into town. I buy Mum a glass owl. Afterwards browse at Hettlage Fashion House where a polo-neck sweater and a vest catch my eye as must haves. Afterwards it's time for the coach trip to Hinterzarten. The hiking route takes us past the ski jump and we get to watch some skiers training. It looks daunting to me, not something I would want to engage in. The hike continues on a lovely forest path. We return to the resort along Lake Titisee which makes the train trip very special. I eat supper in my room. A nurse comes to see me afterwards to ask me how the blister is that I got from wearing my new pair of shoes on Friday. I had asked for a plaster in the morning. I find it refreshing that a doctor or nurse will always have time to talk to me. They will simply come by and ask how things are going. It usually turns into a chat that can last up to 15 minutes. The patient care offered here is really exceptional.

Sunday, 4th September, Medical Wellness Resort Day 12: This morning my brother Franz gets hold of me finally. He will not be coming to visit because they are leaving to go on holiday in the Bavarian Forest on 10th September. A detour here or the return trip via Freiburg would be too far after all. What a pity

but I can understand it. We talk for almost half an hour. It is
such a treat.

My telephone conversations with Gisela have gone a long way in strengthening my faith in her quick recovery. I head off to Freiburg full of anticipation. Gisela waves to me from the window while I park my car in the expansive car park. Moments later we are in one another's arms overjoyed. The rehabilitative resort comes across more like a four-star hotel than a clinic. I am pleasantly surprised after the clinic in Cologne, which essentially would also be able to achieve the same atmosphere if it were to invest in some cheerful décor, pictures on the walls and more natural light in the passages. I am so pleased that this is possible and thrilled that Gisela has struck it this lucky. We go to her room which is equally airy and vibrant and a second bed awaits me. Making it possible for partners to spend the night in a patient's room is another plus point that I am definitely going to award the clinic's management with.

I could immediately see from that special glow in Gisela's eyes that she was doing well. My heart missed a beat I was so happy. She showed me around Freiburg, I liked the city a lot and we would catch the bus to surrounding areas for long walks. The weekend simply flew by and before we knew it we were saying our farewells. If the truth be told, I would much prefer to have stayed on. On the drive home there was a lot to think over. I lifted my gaze to the heavens: "Please dear

God, keep Gisela in your care so that she remains healthy. Thank you that she is doing so well and that she is being taken care of at such a good clinic."

A further unexpected piece of joy would come in the form of my daughter Ramona, now aged eighteen, moving into a flat in the town neighbouring mine. This meant being able to meet up whenever the opportunity presented itself and with it came many a good conversation. Aside from that, every fortnight my son Markus would come to stay with me for the weekend. We would visit my parents and always find something to keep us busy.

The time had come to get the flat into tip-top shape. I did the laundry, ironing and changed the bedding. At 2:30 pm I was already waiting on the platform impatiently, although Gisela's train was only scheduled on the hour. I could not wait to hold her in my arms again. Half an hour felt like an eternity. Then finally the train rolled in brakes squealing. One second I was craning my neck to see if I could spot her, the next I was running towards her, overjoyed to hold her in my arms again. Gisela looked the picture of good health. Now I could look forward to going back to the flat again for a change and true to form, as before our dear neighbours had a welcome home poem stuck to the front door awaiting Gisela:

Luminosity
Sadly when you look outside your door
all you might see is an empty hallway floor.

Momentarily you feel uptight, upset
when all it takes is: One bold step.
As if on cue, a door opens up
a ray of sunshine lifts you up.
Two luminous eyes that know your strife
reviving you with the quintessential light of life.
Even if your heart is dark
let their laughter leave its mark.

Today it is time for a redress,
so let us imbue you with a certain lightness.
For even through your darkest hour
our friendship has miraculous power.
Loving thoughts abound, erupt
boundlessly to light you up.
So that glowing bright once again
will be that ray with Gisela's name.

This poem is a symbol of the strength our friendship radiates. Take all you need for this is a flame that never blows out.

Sandra und Daniel

We stood outside our front door speechless taking in the touching words. Once inside I had a few little surprises in store for Gisela. Often it was the small thoughtful gestures that we would delight one another with, not least of which a note on the kitchen table that would read: "I love you" or "How good that you are here!"

8 Don't give up

On Saturday we took the train to Cologne and treated ourselves to a sumptuous breakfast. Afterwards we lingered at our favourite bookstore then went to browse in a few more shops and had a good lunch before heading home. Gisela was visibly exhausted from the outing. She spent most of the following day in bed reading her new book. I was desperate for some fresh air and took a long walk in the forest.

Gisela was so tense the next morning, her anxiety was palpable. I took her in my arms to comfort her. After breakfast I drove her to the hospital. While they were examining her, my anxiety got the better of me, the magazines in the waiting room were a blur and did little to distract me. It felt like an eternity before Gisela would emerge from the white door. She was pale. Ten minutes later we found ourselves in the oncologist's consulting room. She showed us a fractured rib on an X-ray and a shadow the size of a ripe cherry that she was not yet able to diagnose at that point in time. We remained silent for a long time. All that the doctor, who came across as friendly could tell us, was that further examinations were needed to obtain greater clarity, then with a forced smile swiftly dismissed us, leaving us dumfounded.

Around that time, since on the whole Gisela's health was reasonable in relative terms, she expressed the wish to be able spend time in a warmer climate over December. The idea could not be more welcome. The cold and damp German winter climate was a far cry from conducive to her well-being. After some advice from our friendly travel agent we decided on a fortnight on Gran Canaria. The Canary Islands can be reached by air in as few as four hours from Germany and thanks to the preferential attention the island country receives from the Gulf Stream, its temperatures also prove to be pleasant in winter. Depending on how Gisela felt while away we were planning to extend our stay by a few more days when there.

Gran Canaria spoiled us with no shortage of sunshine and our holiday apartment was equally appealing. All that Gisela wanted to do was to be able to give free rein to her thoughts, her days oscillating between reading and relaxation as her preferred pastimes. Occasionally we would go for a walk and enjoy the warmth of the sun. On some days we would go on a small outing to explore the island and its people. The sunny island was growing on us. Gran Canaria, which I had visited for the first time 14 years earlier, came as an unexpected surprise to Gisela in what it had to offer. Of course there were many unappealing tourist complexes, but they were eyesores that the sandy beaches that stretched on forever and the panoramic view of the ocean would make up for.

Despite a suspected fractured rib which Gisela incurred thanks to the effects of a heavy sneeze on such a frail body, we extended the trip to mid-January. Even so, it was becoming blatantly apparent that our days on Gran Canaria were numbered. We would have given anything to stay on but Cologne awaited us and we had to go back. With it came the prospect of less pleasant temperatures, which in hindsight were of course the least of our worries.

Numerous job applications later, I finally got hired at a printing house in Leverkusen. On the one hand I was pleased to have found gainful employment once again; on the other it meant I would have less time for Gisela from now on. She was now receiving Aredia infusions at Rainer's practice. More medical examinations were in the pipeline. I had to be at work and on the day they were scheduled I could not unfortunately accompany her to the hospital. At work it played on my mind and I kept sending prayers to our dear God. At long last it was time to knock off in the late afternoon and I drove home with a nagging sense of unease. Gisela greeted me with sad eyes. A second rib had suffered a fracture and a further shadow had become discernible on the X-ray. The doctors had scheduled new appointments for her. It was infuriating. The feeling of helplessness was the worst. It made me angry. A merciless interplay of hopes and fears was deciding on our fate!

Gisela was now crying more frequently, would tell me more often that she did not want to die. That she was too young to die. I tried to console her and begged her not to give up, whatever happened. For a long time Gisela did not tell me about the lump she had felt in the region of her rib. Rainer arranged for an appointment at the clinic in Cologne. I took time off work and accompanied her on the next difficult step to hospital where Gisela had to have a skin metastases removed as an outpatient.

The intervention was followed by a sonographic examination of the abdomen, a chest X-ray, a sonography of the axilla, a CAT scan of the abdomen, a CAT scan of the skull and the thorax. The subsequent findings confirmed the doctors' suspicions that we were dealing with a bone metastases in the rib area. Where Gisela still managed to gain the strength from to deal with this less than inspiring information, was beyond my comprehension. The doctors ran through the chances of a cure with chemotherapy and radiation with us at great length. This time they also spoke of alternative healing methods.

Once back home, Gisela cried her eyes out, vented her pain screaming out loud and was asking for her brother. I rang Franz and less than half an hour later he was on the doorstep. Her brother was the hero of the day. Somehow he was able to take his sister's mind off the pressing issues looming over her and managed to fill the day with welcome distractions. Over the next few days while with him, we visited our parents and Ramona, went to the cinema with Markus and met up with friends and colleagues over lunch.

Franz suggested that his sister see a naturopath in Bonn. After all, in a situation like this no effort should be spared. Dr Schuppert recommended thymus and mistletoe therapy, as well as an ozone autologous treatment. After a consultation with him a smidgeon of hope had returned to Gisela's eyes. From now on she had to go to Bonn three times a week for the applications, which kept her motivated.

Since the physicians in Freiburg had been more open to alternative curative treatments by far compared to their colleagues in Cologne, Gisela asked Rainer to arrange an impatient admission at the Freiburg Clinic for her. After countless phone calls and faxes he finally succeeded in getting an opening for her. Rainer was invaluable to Gisela. This was a guy who would do anything in his power for her.

Four weeks later I drove to Freiburg with Gisela. The room she was allocated was light and friendly, just as was the case during the time already spent at the Medical Wellness Resort which formed part of the same clinic. Only now she was in a different wing, which also explained why we would invariably come across patients who were visibly ill. When I walked past them I instinctively said a silent prayer that somehow they would get well soon. On the lonely drive home I prayed and prayed.

Gisela stayed a week. After a series of thorough examinations the doctors prescribed irradiation therapy and further Aredia infusions as a treatment. She had already received the first infusion in Freiburg. Back home Gisela told me that the doctors had put her remaining life expectation at six months. Whether this was with the radiation treatment or without remained an unknown for us.

After her return home, Gisela again drove to Bonn where she was to receive the Aredia infusions. Dr Schuppert recommended a clinic in Bonn to help her along. They had an appointment for her in mid-May. The outcome: Recommended assessment by a hospital that was more specialised in her medical condition. Rainer made the arrangements and she got an appointment at short notice. The specialist clinic examined her thoroughly. She needed to come back a week later by which time the results would be available and the cancer could then be treated in a target-orientated approach.

Seven days had since elapsed. Gisela and I found ourselves in the treatment room in front of a brightly lit screen to which four X-rays had been stuck. It was an awful scenario; the images made me feel scared beyond compare. Using his index finger, the Head Physician delineated the bone metastases in the vicinity of the ribs. He gave us a detailed explanation how metastases are formed and the course of action that can be taken against them. There was a clinic in Cologne that offered selective irradiation with state-of-the-art equipment thereby making for effective treatment while at the same time going easy on the other organs. Once the treatment in Cologne had been completed, they could continue with a chemotherapy treatment in Münster, a two-and-a-half hour drive from Cologne. After thoroughly weighing up the road ahead, Gisela decided on the irradiation therapy. Admittedly it was something she would normally not have considered, but with the tables regarding her future having turned so dramatically, she was now determined to leave no stone unturned to prolong her life.

After the consultation for the irradiation therapy Gisela showed me the blue markings on the skin on her stomach. She told me she was afraid of the treatment. A week after her 41st birthday she had to leave for Cologne to have her first session. She felt dreadful afterwards and told me: "If I only have a few more months to live, the last place I want to spend them is in the lavatory throwing up. I want to make the most of the time I have left. Perhaps there is yet hope for a miracle."

9 Heidenhäuschen

It was at my new job that I got to know Carla. Somewhere in the course of our conversations I told her about Gisela's illness. It turned out that Carla's brother was a life coach and nutritionist and she recommended that we contact him for advice. By chance he was going to be doing a talk in Cologne soon, which spared us the drive to the town of Hadamar near Limburg where he lived which was all of 100 kilometres south-east of Cologne in the direction of Frankfurt

So it turned out that on one Tuesday evening Gisela and I were sitting in a well-lit conference room together with 25 or so other interested individuals as Carla's brother Lothar and his wife Nadine, a therapist and nurse, presented us with a lecture on healthy nutrition and lifestyle. And on the fundamental role this can play in maintaining optimal health, and in the case of the prevalence of illness, how it can contribute towards recovery. During the lecture I realised how crucial this subject was to Gisela. That evening we had a long conversation with Lothar and Nadine.

The week that followed I was overcome with an unusual sense of unease, which seemed to get worse as the week progressed. I kept thinking of Lothar and Nadine in this context and put two and two together. Realising there had to be a connection I told Gisela what I had been feeling. Her instantaneous response was: "Why don't we go and see them next weekend?"

Without giving it a second thought I phoned Nadine who assured me that we were very welcome.

When we stepped into Lothar and Nadine's flat we immediately sensed the warm atmosphere that greeted us. We spoke for a long time about a healthy lifestyle, illness, death and healing. About what one could do against cancer via nutrition and about alternative medicine! Gisela and I got plenty of new ideas and invaluable new knowledge. Afterwards we all went for dinner at a country guest house, which also happened to be where we were booked for the night.

Once Lothar and Nadine had said their farewells, we went for a walk. It was a mild evening, not a hint of a breeze, the fresh smell of the soil rising into my nostrils unmistakably reminding me of my childhood. In the distance we noticed a small mountain surrounded by a mixed forest interspersed by a few houses. Impulsively we decided to explore the area in the morning.

We took our time over breakfast, went over the subjects discussed the day before and the new insights gleaned. The meeting had left its invaluable imprint on us. When we paid the bill, the owner was kind enough to give us detailed instructions on how to get to our next destination, all the while singing the praises of the lookout point on the small mountain called Heidenhäuschen.

We parked our car in the village of Oberzeuzheim and slowly made our way uphill in a forest area. I noticed that Gisela had trouble walking. A few hundred metres on we discovered a stream right in the middle of the forest and a sign near it said: "Seven sorrows – Seven joys". We would learn later on that it referred to a catholic sanctuary established here in 1885 when healing powers had been ascribed to the waters of the stream. Placed alongside the stream were some Thank You plaques which read: "Thank you Virgin Mary," "Mary who has come to my aide" and "Thank you for healing me." Placed before a wooden cross were several benches that invited pilgrims to prayer. We sat down and listened to the song of the birds permeating the sunlit clearing. Gisela leant against my shoulder. I took her in my arms and prayed to God that this wonderful person could somehow be cured.

We carried on our hike across well laid out forest paths until we reached the lookout point at a height of 400 metres. The hair on my arms stood on end on observing the numerous pieces of rock strewn across the forest giving the place a mystical touch. Everything looked so familiar to me, yet I was utterly certain that it was my first ever visit to this spot. A two by two metre natural structure of grey stone gave the impression of an altar, or even a sacrificial altar. I told Gisela about the strange sensations I was getting. We embraced and kissed one another. I felt a deep love for her. It became crystal clear to me that my thoughts defined my life. Gisela too had come to this revelation. She now strongly felt the cancer had no right to control her. We stood there a long time holding one another tight, let the view into the distance captivate us. This spot was the epitome of peace and quiet... it felt timeless.

On the route back I read on one of the information boards that the Celts had once conquered this place. Could it have been a sacred site? *The Celts*, strangely it was a word that would trigger something unexplained in me, as if wanting to share something infinitely significant with me. The only thing was that whatever this was, it came across as blurred, distant and unattainable. Somehow it boded the future, but also captured the past, was alive in the here and now: *The Celts*.

On the return hike Gisela was a few metres ahead of me on the narrow path. I got the fright of my life when she suddenly burst into loud crying and screaming and rushed to her. Once she had calmed down somewhat, she said she had seen a pine tree wrapped in a gleaming bright light. It was truly eerie and sent a chill down my spine. Once more my hair stood up inexplicably. *What was going down here?* We continued on our way slowly, now holding one another by the hand. The weirdest mood had overcome me. Something about Gisela had changed. Her step had changed noticeably from the climb up. It was lighter!

"You know what, Mano, the pain has gone," she said when we had reached the car. Her face was beaming with sheer elation. "The pain is gone," she screamed. She began to sob and held me tight. On the drive home we could not help wondering about the out of the ordinary events of the past few days. It had now become clear to me why we had to come to Hadamar. I had so hoped that Lothar and Nadine could somehow help Gisela. Miracles do happen and as from that day I believed in them once more.

Back at work I told Carla about our special weekend, about the experiences we had had, the conversations and the new realisations. She was happy for Gisela, who decided to make her way to Lothar and Nadine once more later that week, so convinced was she that they were instrumental in helping her on the road to health. In the afternoon she fetched me from work. She did not have to say much, her expression spoke volumes. The visit had evidently proved to be beneficial for her. From now on she would go for a treatment session at Hadamar once a week. New hope sprung up in our lives. The Aredia infusions that Rainer was administering likewise appeared to give her a new lease on life. And in Bonn she would continue to receive her other treatments. She literally did everything to keep the cancer in check and to try to conquer it.

Gisela remained upbeat; consciously chose to dress in vibrant colours, invested in a new hairstyle, met up with friends and focussed her thoughts on wellness and life. We treated the warm summer days as an open invitation to do our favourite things. We drove to Cologne and took long walks along the River Rhine when we did not have other commitments, listened to live music and dined at our favourite restaurants.

My attitude to life had changed. I saw things from a different perspective. Things that had been important to me in the past no longer had any significance. If you think about it, what is really important about life? Health had attained a very high priority for me. I recognised how valuable it was to go through life without physical pain, without debilitation. Yes, to be awarded that privilege. It is the little things in life that bring us great happiness on earth. A smile from Gisela made me happy. I would give up all the money and gold on this earth for her health.

10 Fasting therapy

Richard, a former work colleague of Gisela's, had invited us to his birthday. Over coffee and cake we also spoke about Gisela's medical condition, with Richard telling us about a friend who runs a health centre in the German Central Uplands of Hunsrück, approximately a two-hour drive south of Cologne in the direction of Wiesbaden. It turns out that she is a facilitator of the so-called Breuss fasting therapy, named after the early 20th century Austrian healer, Rudolph Breuss, who developed it.

Richard, very conversant with the topic, filled us in on what he knew about it. The treatment is based on the principle that a cancerous tumour is an autonomous growth. Nourished by protein, the proliferation of the tumour occurs, as does the degeneration of the surrounding area. This can however be circumvented since it is possible for the cells of such a growth to starve and be eaten up if subjected to an organic vegetable juice regimen. This can be achieved with the Breuss fasting therapy, a fresh vegetable juice diet as it were, which ensures that the body no longer receives any protein from outside. Since realistically the organism cannot survive without this substance, the protein-hungry blood helps itself to and feasts on all superfluous growths and tumours in the body. As a result the cancer is eaten up by the body itself. Essentially this is the equivalent of an operation, except without the deployment of a scalpel.

The fasting therapy must be strictly adhered to for 42 days for it to be effective and during that time the patient may not partake in any solids. The Breuss juice is essentially comprised of beetroot, carrots, celeriac, radishes and potatoes. As well as special herbal teas. Rudolf Breuss in his book *The Breuss Cancer Cure* claims to have cured more than 40,000 cancer patients with this therapy.

If one is to go by the prognosis of the doctors in Freiburg, Gisela would die in two months. Dr Schuppert in Bonn had recommended a fever-chemotherapy. Gisela wanted to find out more about the fasting therapy and then reach a decision.

A further week had gone by. I had taken off work and found myself in the waiting room of a Cologne surgeon. Gisela was having four skin metastases removed as an outpatient. The thought of what she had to go through made me feel nauseous: "Dear God how is it possible for one person to have to suffer so much?" I felt like screaming at the top of my voice. With Gisela's health having deteriorated dramatically I now only worked half day. Since I could not do anything other than pray and comfort her, a boundless rage was stirring inside of me.

The next day she had to go back to Cologne to see a doctor. Twice en route I had to stop the car, she was feeling so nauseous that she had to vomit. I turned the car around. Back home Gisela went straight to bed. I phoned Rainer, who appeared a short while later and prescribed painkillers. Gisela confided in him telling him she wanted to die. Could he give her something that would finally put her to sleep? Her friend had no choice but to deny her such a fate, it was not within his permissible scope to engage in assisted suicide. On Gisela's request I cancelled all of her doctors' appointments.

After careful thought Gisela decided on the fasting therapy. On Saturday, 28th October we made our way to the Hunsrück region. Gisela immediately felt at ease at Adele Becker's treatment centre. It was tranquil and light, there was an atmosphere of recovery about the centre. The décor in her room was warm with a generous view of the autumnal mixed forest. Adele Becker explained the procedure to us.

It involved drinking small quantities of different liquids at different times of the day. No bed rest is necessary during the treatment. It is best to be as active as possible and provide distractions from any hunger pangs and prevailing illness.

Before commencing the fasting therapy, it was recommended that Gisela first recuperate by gaining new strength from food grown organically to build up her system. Then there was the foot reflexology, the lymph drainage sessions, colon cleansing, daily yoga and meditation classes that would restore her inner peace and balance.

After any questions that we still had were answered I went with Gisela to her room and promised that I would come to her immediately whenever she needed me. Gisela soon became friends with Adele, the staff and the other people who were booked into the centre. They would go for walks in the forest together and learnt to welcome the peace and isolation. In the evenings they would have long conversations. My darling was beginning to feel better by the day, so much so that soon she was able to get relief using natural pain killers only.

At the weekend I visited Gisela with Markus. She looked great. However, I did notice that her movements were sluggish and cautious. She was pleased that I had brought with me Markus who was patiently drawing a picture of the landscape while I listened to all of her news. After lunch I had a long chat with Adele, who sounded optimistic about Gisela's recovery. Even so, when I drove home late that afternoon it was with mixed feelings.

I sent the following letter to Gisela a few days later:

My Darling!

My thoughts are with you all day every day. I love you and there is nothing that I could wish for more fervently but for you to get well again and be pain-free. It is hard for me just to sit there unable to do anything and watch you suffering in pain. When I look back on our time together it makes me happy that we always stuck together. Even if it was not always easy! We have been together almost seven years. It has been a fascinating, loving, exciting and enlightening time. The best and most valuable thing about it is however our loyalty to one another and that we can always depend on one another.

It still makes me sad that I have not always been as I would have liked to have been. That is happy, satisfied and cheerful. Regrettably there were circumstances occasionally that led to my being sad and unhappy at times. Today I am the wiser for it. And these experiences will guide us into a new, beautiful and happy future. I have had a lot of time to reflect, read and write in the past few days.

If you live your life in harmony with how it was intended for you, if you focus solely on your health and yourself, I believe better health can be yours again. You are a very special person. You will have seen, particularly since your illness, how many people love you and what loyal friends you have. You can truly be proud of yourself. Also, your parents love you dearly. If they sometimes think and act differently, that is understandable. Our parents cannot always understand us and the reverse is also true. I will phone you tonight. Sending you a thousand kisses.

I love you
Mano

Boundless get well wishes, phone calls and presents from friends were helping Gisela to keep up her strength. Anyhow this is what she had been assuring me on the phone, hence my huge fright when I saw her on my next visit. It was obvious that she had lost a lot of weight and she now only leaves her bed rarely. The health complaints troubling her most were the excruciating pain and visual disturbances. In the course of a longer conversation I tried to find out what Adele's take was on Gisela's condition. She did not yet want to admit that the treatment had failed. I was not the only one who was beginning to have my lingering doubts.

The advent season leading up to Christmas was upon us. The thought of Christmas made me feel sad. In the department store I found the red cashmere jumper that Gisela had had her sights set on for a long time. The soft jumper in hand I made my way to the till and began to cry.

Will my darling ever wear it?

The cashier looked at me a little taken aback, but for once I did not feel any embarrassment at not being able to hold back the tears. As soon I was driving back home in the car I let loose and screamed out in pain with all my might, my body shaking. When I was with Gisela I was able to keep it together. I always managed to stay strong. In these times I realised that we can only be strong if we also give free rein to our weaknesses. Crying had nothing to do with weakness. It is a normal human reaction any person will have. Anyone able to display their feelings is strong in my book.

My telephone conversations with Gisela always put me in a good mood. I looked forward to hearing her voice, even when I could distinctly hear the pain in it, as hard as she tried to conceal this. I drove to Gisela the day before Christmas Eve. My darling wife greeted me with a big smile. I was so happy to be with her and could contain my tears no longer. She gently stroked my face, we held one another tightly and we both cried.

Gisela asked me to help her wash her hair. I helped her to the basin and it cut through me like a knife when I felt how fragile she was. I carefully sat her on a stool in front of the basin. I washed her hair as fast as possible and felt a sense of relief when she was lying back in her bed.

Since Gisela had not been able to leave her bed on her own for days now, Adele was very worried. It was with great difficulty that she had helped her shower. Eventually I told Adele that Gisela would be better off in hospital in the state she was in. I had often pleaded with Gisela to allow me to take her to hospital, but she always refused. After 35 days though, she decided to end the fasting therapy. From then on she ate solids again, at first with great difficulty keeping any food down.

On Christmas Eve I got up early and went to see Gisela, who was still fast asleep. I sat at her bedside and looked her in the face. Moments later she opened her eyes and bestowed a smile on me: "Good morning darling, did you sleep okay?"

"Yes, you cannot help but sleep well in these tranquil surrounds."

I gave her a kiss then went to get us our breakfast. As she lay propped up in bed drinking tea, with me sitting beside her, we started talking about Bali. We relived our first long haul trip together to Thailand. Asia fascinated me and it gave Gisela great delight to be able to share my enthusiasm. After half an hour I could see that talking was making her tired. I tucked her in, went back to my room, donned my hiking boots and made my way into the forest.

It had been snowing a bit. The temperatures were hovering around freezing point. I hiked across the solid ground slowly. The silence was intense. Christmas was tangible. Jesus Christ was born today I thought to myself. Today some 1995 years ago. In that moment in time I had a sense of understanding of eternity... *Death... dying? No, death cannot be the end of everything. I was implicitly certain of this. Was Gisela going to die soon? And if so, what then? Then I would be alone again – just as was the case then. The words of her little advert when we first met echoed in my mind. Hey you! Are you also alone?*

When I got back Gisela was sleeping again, or still sleeping, I went to lie on my bed to read my book. Sometime later, the Christmas presents under my arm I went back to her room. The portable CD player her work colleagues had bought her was a raging success. She was now able to listen to her favourite music and was overjoyed that her colleagues had thought of her. As for the cashmere sweater she held it against her cheek in delight.

"I'm sad I didn't get the chance to get you a gift."

"But I've got you. There is no bigger and more beautiful gift in this world," I comforted her.

Someone was knocking at the door. It was Hannelore, a young woman who was one of the kitchen staff. She asked if she could come in. She handed Gisela a gift and wished her a happy Christmas. The wrapper revealed a small candle and a small bottle of eau de toilette. We were so moved that we both began crying like little children. Taken aback by the unexpected reaction Hannelore said: "I only meant well." Gisela motioned to her that they were tears of joy. Hannelore could not stay long, her family was waiting for her and she still had to cook dinner at home. The gift felt more precious than the most expensive diamond in the world. It contained something priceless that was not comparable to anything – love.

Minutes later there was another knock at the door. It was Gertrude who was staying in the room next door, also with a gift for Gisela. It was a nativity scene the size of a matchbox. We were both deeply moved. Adele and her staff had decorated the common room festively. Four of us carried Gisela up two flights of stairs and lay her down on the couch. Everyone was delighted that she could take part in the festivities and did not have to spend the evening in her room. Among the guests there was an endearing 83-year-old woman who read us a Christmas Tale. She had to interrupt the story a few times while reading because her voice broke down. It was the moving story of her life. She recounted the tough years when there had been very little to eat at Christmas. Gifts, if there were any at all, were modest. We could all feel from the emotion welling up in her as she read, how much sharing her autobiography with us all, meant to her.

It crossed my mind that this could potentially be Gisela's last Christmas. An agonising sadness weighed heavily on my heart. Yet at the same time I would not let go of the belief that a miracle could still happen. I simply was not going to give up. I had consciously decided to live every moment with Gisela as though it were my last.

We sang Christmas carols, drank copious pots of tea and indulged in delicious Christmas bakes. The feeling was unanimous, not one of us had ever experienced Christmas Eve with so much depth of feeling. Every now and again Gisela's eyes would fall closed. Later we carefully took her to bed. I stayed with her until she fell asleep, gave her a kiss and went to my room.

Early on Christmas Day I got up and immediately made my way to her room. She was still fast asleep when I entered. I took a chair, placed it alongside the bed and looked at her. She looked like an angel. It took a while for her to open her eyes. "Mano, I love you so much," were her first words. I sat on her bed, she gently stroked my cheek. "I love you so much, my darling," I whispered softly in her ear.

The expression in her eyes had transformed. They radiated wisdom and love, touched me deeply to the core. Concealed inside them was eternity. *Was she preparing herself? Had she come to this tranquil place to take leave?* We had not excluded death from our conversations and what would follow. It was the kind of openness that I was sure would cushion the blow of death, farewell and loss for us both, albeit negligibly.

Gisela lost twelve kilograms. Nobody knew what her insides looked like. Despite the painkillers which she had been taking regularly for some days now again, I could see she was in pain. I strongly urged her to agree to go to a hospital. Adele told me that aside from providing her with a regeneration diet and nursing her, there was very little else she could still do for her.

I would have given anything to take Gisela home with me when it was time for me to leave again, but it was not to be. Her condition would not allow it. On the drive home, a strange sense of peace overcame me. The streets were empty, making the trip comfortable. The glimpses of decorated Christmas trees inside people's homes gave me a sense of security, yet at the same time the world around me was beginning to feel increasingly unreal.

It was cold inside our flat, just as it was inside of me. After I had turned on all the heaters I made a number of phone calls. The very next day I went straight to Rainer who suggested I have Gisela taken to a hospital. Fortunately she agreed but did not want to be fetched in an ambulance. Our friend Richard, who had first introduced us to fasting therapy, came to the rescue and agreed to fetch her in his minibus. He would remove the back seat and place a mattress inside. I did not like the idea at all because I knew how fragile Gisela had become. Even the smallest lapse in attention on the part of the driver could mean she could break more bones. In the end I respected Gisela's wish and on New Year's Day made my way to Hunsrück with Richard.

The winter had taken its toll on the road and it meant that we got there much later than expected. I dressed Gisela warmly and made sure she was wrapped up snugly. It was bitterly cold. To add to our existing woes we had to climb down a long slippery staircase. It meant holding Gisela between us, taking one painstaking step at a time until we reached the car below. It felt like an eternity to me before we finally had Gisela lying on the mattress. Richard was a star. He had thought of everything: Water, plastic bag, bed sheets, pillows and blankets.

After a drive that took more than three hours we finally reached the flat. I unlocked the front door. There were still more stairs to negotiate since we lived on the second floor. Finally, with combined forces and plenty of patience we managed to carry Gisela to her bed. It was past midnight.

11 Love is never ending

The following morning I phoned Rainer. Not even 15 minutes had elapsed and he was already standing by Gisela's bed deep in thought. An hour later she was on her way to hospital in an ambulance. Rainer had to attend to his practice. I phoned work to let my employer know what had transpired and asked to take another day's leave. I packed a small overnight case for Gisela and made my way to her. After a series of thorough examinations the treating physician told me that she had become extremely dehydrated because of the fasting treatment during which time she was evidently not drinking enough water hence weakening her system. Gisela was allocated a room with two beds. In the afternoon Franz, his wife Anne and her parents were the first to come by.

I had been able to extend my three-week leave by a week. This meant I was able to be at Gisela's side. By now she was hardly eating any solid foods and drinking very little. She could hardly keep anything down of the little she ate and was being given fluids intravenously to prevent her body from dehydrating completely. Gisela never ceased to amaze the doctors, nurses and patients around her. Despite the advanced stage of her illness she would always make an effort to smile.

After two weeks in hospital the doctors informed us that other than alleviating the pain, there was very little else they could still do. The announcement had a ring of finality to it and I felt scared. They recommended that she be transferred to a palliative ward at the Bensberg Rehabilitation Clinic near Cologne. This was similar to a hospice. It was where patients, to whom it was humanly impossible to give any further medical treatment, were transferred to, to be given end-of-life care. There they were called guests. Gisela's parents tried to convince their daughter that this was best for her.

Sister Lydia, a co-worker at the palliative facility came to visit Gisela to tell her more about the ward: A maximum of six patients were allocated to two rooms at a time, the atmosphere was friendly and the doctors, nurses and caseworkers looked after the patients caringly. I liked Sister Lydia from the very first moment.

It was on the 15th January that Gisela was transferred to the palliative ward of the Bensberg Rehabilitation Clinic. The facility was exactly as Sister Lydia had described it. Light friendly rooms with a view across the spectacular garden. Wherever possible, the patients were granted their every wish.

Gisela now received regular morphine injections for pain and she slept a lot, during the day. We reduced the number of visitors to give her more peace. Gisela's face was aging visibly. She was no longer able to take in any solid foods and all she would consume in a day were a few spoons of tea. Her swollen arms were preventing the doctors from hydrating her with any further transfusions through her veins. Her fluid retention was extreme yet the doctors decided against tapping. They did not want to cause Gisela any unnecessary hardship.

"Mano, I want to die," she confided in me when we were alone. "And please let everybody know they mustn't wear black to my funeral." I promised her I would make sure of it.

That same evening I had a long conversation with Dr Merkel, the Head Physician of the palliative ward. He tried to convey to me as sensitively as possible the reality that my wife would in all likelihood die in the next few days. I broke down crying. Finally the last glimmer of hope had been ripped from me. Dr Merkel, aside from being an excellent doctor, was also very empathetic human being: "I have seldom come across a human being like your wife. Even in the darkest hours of her illness she is still able to spare a smile or friendly word," he said full of genuine admiration.

"She's such a wonderful person. Is it true that we can no longer hold out hope? I simply cannot conceive of her dying."

"I'm so sorry. It will take a miracle to save her now…"

It took me a long time before I was able to articulate something to say. Then I told Dr Merkel about Christel Zachert's book. *We will meet again in my paradise.*

"Do you know something, I get the distinct impression that it was not by chance that this book happened to come my way. Of all days, it was on the day that they found an anomaly in my wife's armpit during a routine examination, that I found an advert for the book in a magazine at the dentist's. I even went to buy myself a copy straight afterwards. I'm convinced that the book prepared me for the things that were beginning to unfold in my life at that time. My wife and I have often spoken about death. We both believe that death is not an end in itself."

Dr Merkel agreed with me, "It is also my strong conviction. Sometimes things happen for which there is no plausible explanation. Some of my experiences in the palliative ward are definitely testimony to the fact that things can happen for which there is no logical explanation that is humanly possible."

After my conversation with Dr Merkel, I went to Gisela and told her what he had said. I could not help crying and she stroked my face comfortingly. Once I had gathered myself I spoke to her softly: "Your life is a beautiful mosaic, from which only a few pieces are still missing. Once the missing pieces are added to it, then the picture forming the mosaic is complete." While I spoke to her, it felt as though Gisela was on the path to perfection.

That same evening I made a few phone calls. My sister-in-law Claudia did not want to miss out on seeing Gisela one last time and came to the hospital right away the next morning. Gisela was overjoyed at Claudia's visit. They were good friends. Claudia and Gisela had a lot in common. She too was an attractive and intelligent woman and with her friendliness a blessing for her fellow human beings. She served the community in her invaluable role as a nurse at the intensive care unit in the town of Frechen bordering on Cologne. The two women held each other tightly for a long time. Repairing to the kitchen, I left them to be alone to help with the washing up, which I would do every now and again, and to be honest it was good to have someone to talk to and lend me a listening ear.

I had promised Gisela that I would get hold of an eye patch for her since her vision in her left eye had become blurred and she wanted to cover it. I walked into town with Claudia, there was a nip in the air. It was reassuring to know I could rely on my sister-in-law who was making herself available day and night during this difficult time in case I needed her help. I was infinitely grateful. Even in the past she had helped me through difficult situations with her good advice. I count my blessings in having such an amazing friend.

With Gisela still asleep when we got back to her room, we went to sit at a table in the passage and spoke about life and death. Every so often a nurse in passing would come and sit with us for a few minutes to join in the conversation. I realised that every time I was able to talk about my feelings and my pain, I would get a sense of relief. We spoke about people who believe in God, those who believe in eternal life or rebirth and reincarnation. For Gisela, death did not mean finality, but rather a transition into another life. Whatever form this may take.

I was becoming increasingly aware of how important a palliative care ward was for a dying person. People spend the last days of their life in it. Death is so often associated with fear and pain. The team here make it their mission to alleviate some of that fear and pain and were always ready to engage in conversation with the patient or their loved ones. The extraordinary nurses and doctors, who care for the people in such a touching manner, inadvertently give the dying person a sense of dignity. They treat the dying with love and respect. In the past people would die at home surrounded by close family – death was part of life. Sadly often today the dying are ostracised. Illness and death have no place in our pleasure-seeking society, which is a contradiction in terms anyway because surely treating your fellow human being in such a degrading manner cannot be fun at all.

When we were back in Gisela's ward, she asked me if her legs were lying in the right position. For days she could no longer move them on her own. An open bedsore had formed on her back. The morphine meant that she was pain-free, as Dr Merkel had promised me. I liked how the people running the ward decided on how to deal with each patient. In the early evening Claudia said her farewells when Franz and Anne arrived. Gisela smiled at her one last time. They both knew this was goodbye... for good!

In the next few days the doctors were astonished to see Gisela have quite an appetite, 'tucking' into yoghurt and mashed potato with gravy. I had not seen her eat like this in a long time. It was a joy to behold. When I asked the doctors what they thought, they said it was not unusual for something like this to happen. She also drank more fluids, which she was even able to do on her own with the help of a straw.

Even though this was a time of intense sadness for me, there were also so many beautiful moments in these hours. We held each others hands and stroked one another's skin, seeking solace in one another. Gisela looked at me surprised when I told her: "You are beautiful." "Really?" she asked. Obviously her medical condition had left its mark. Yet on the inside, to me, it was as though she was becoming more beautiful by the day.

The end of January had arrived. It was cold and wet outside. It snowed on some days. In between being with Gisela I went for walks, being out in nature helped me to regain some strength. Life and death were part of nature. Every second a living creature or organism was being born and every second one was dying also. Life, death, life, death – a perpetual cycle without a beginning and without an end. Without death there would be no birth, without birth no death. Surely death could not be something final. There is much more to it that we human beings with our limited understanding cannot grasp.

My leave had come to an end. On the Monday morning I got up at seven thirty. Ironically suddenly I was the one who felt like death warmed up, I felt tired and exhausted. The past few months had sapped all my energy. I could not and did not want to go to work. Anyway Gisela had taken up my mind completely. She needed me by her side, it was more important than work and all the money in the world. I decided to go and see Rainer in his practice. After examining me he confirmed that I was not in great shape health-wise. He said it was not surprising in my situation. He wrote me a sick note.

Before I drove to the hospital I bought some white orchids at the florist. Gisela was still sleeping so I placed the flowers in a vase and chatted with her parents until she woke up. Gisela loved the orchids; she was so happy that I could be by her side.

Every evening after work Gisela's brother came to visit his sister. On the one visit he brought with him a book by the popular late 19th century German satirical author Wilhelm Busch, best known for his humoristic tales in rhyming verses about the prankster lads 'Max and Moritz' who would get up to all kinds of mischief. Franz's reading sessions soon became an evening institution of sorts, the two women sharing Gisela's room having become keen listeners also.

Sadly Gisela's condition worsened. Dr Merkel told me in confidence that she could die any day now. Gisela had already discussed her funeral ceremony and cremation with her parents. The casket with her ashes should be buried at a cemetery close to where her parents lived. Her mother asked me if I was in agreement with the arrangements. It went without saying that I was, I would never want to go against what they had decided among themselves.

Gisela gave me precise instructions what she wanted to wear for the cremation: Her colourful summer dress, her favourite earrings, the soft woollen cardigan and her red shoes. The dress was still in the clean laundry basket, which meant it needed ironing. That evening I set up the ironing board, waited for the iron to get hot and got on with the task at hand. You are ironing the dress your wife is going to wear at her cremation ceremony and you are not flipping out, were the thoughts that ran through my head. She had looked simply captivating in that dress. I felt utterly miserable and was glad when I had finished ironing. The job was not perfect to be honest, I still noticed some creases.

I took the items of clothing and drove with them to the hospital the next morning. It was the twelfth of February. A woman in Gisela's room had sadly passed away and the other patient, who was feeling a little better had been moved to another ward. I had promised Gisela to be at her side when she died and hold her hand. An eerie sensation came over me when I realised that 17th February the day we had met for the first time seven years ago, was just around the corner.

By now Gisela was hardly able to take in any food or water. Her unusual beauty increasingly reminded me of the wood carving from Bali. I realised that Gisela's face began to resemble the sculpture more and more. All efforts at denial were failing me. Fact of the matter, this was as real as it could get. At some point in time I began to accept what was happening. Gisela spent most of her time sleeping. I sat by her side, time went into oblivion for me, it had lost all meaning. After all, what is time?

12 Seven years

"Mano, will you take my ashes to Bali?" Gisela asked me.

"I thought you and your parents had already agreed to an urn grave near their house?"

"Yes I did, but on second thoughts I want to be taken to Bali. I already asked Franz and he has agreed to the idea."

"Do you have somewhere specific in Bali in mind, my darling?"

"Yes, at the waterfall we visited with Bärbel and Klaus."

I felt a chill run down my spine.

"One more thing Mano, be sure to take Franz with you. You won't get by with your level of English."

That evening I had a chat with Franz who assured me he would do everything humanly possible to fulfil his sister's last wish. The next day he was already sending faxes to the German and Indonesian embassies in Bali. I could not recollect where exactly the waterfall was located. On giving it some thought it occurred to me that it had to be somewhere in the north of Bali, not far from Singaraja.

I found myself staring at and admiring the face of the wooden carving which I had acquired at Gisela's last wish waterfall of all places. Unbelievable! I shook my body, as though that would somehow rid me of the pent-up tension cutting through me. That is what electricity current impulses must feel like, I thought to myself. I let my body sink into an armchair, still captivated by the flawless beauty made of wood standing before me. Was it really only by chance that she had chosen the spot where I had bought the statue to be laid to rest? She had travelled the whole world. There were an infinite number of possibilities of places to be laid to rest that she could have chosen: Leverkusen where we had our flat, Leipzig her city of birth or near her parents. But it had to be at the waterfall in question.

I could not help becoming deeply absorbed in thinking about our mysterious connections with this waterfall. In December 1993 on the recommendation of our driver John we had driven to the waterfall *by chance*. It was there that I acquired a wood carving that I felt drawn to as if magically. For some strange reason, back home every now and again the sight of it would send a shiver down my spine. I had a feeling that it was concealing some or other hidden secret. Two-and-a-half years later Gisela, aware that she was dying, expressed the wish to be laid to rest at the same place where I had bought the sculpture, a sculpture whose face resembled hers in uncanny likeness −.

Since Gisela now had the room to herself, we decided to take it in turns to stay by her side overnight. The doctors and nurses here must definitely be applauded for their flexible and helpful attitude. Once again they came through for us and gave us all the support we needed in this situation. I spent the first night at Gisela's side. She awoke twice in the night asking for something to drink. Since she was no longer able to drink with a straw on her own, I took a swab and as the nurses had suggested, dipped it in water and gave it to her. During the night, the night nurse came by once to give her a pain-relieving injection. I lay awake for a long time, I simply could not fall asleep, glancing across to Gisela every so often. *This cannot be. I am lying here awaiting the death of my wife. Listening out for every breath she takes. Startled by any change in her breathing. Aware of every sound.* The wind was whistling through the cracks in the window. From time to time the passage would light up red, followed by an acoustic signal. Endless thoughts went through my head. At six in the morning I looked at the clock. Sister Helene came into the room.

"Good morning is everything fine?" she asked.

"Yes, she is sleeping."

An overwhelming fatigue suddenly overcame me. When I opened my eyes again, I looked at Gisela's face.

"Good morning, my darling."

"Good morning, my darling," I replied, got up and gave her a kiss.

"Did you sleep well?" she asked me.

"Not much, but well."

Sister Helene came to give Gisela another injection. I took the opportunity to go to the bathroom then went to the kitchen. Sister Lydia had brewed a fresh pot of coffee. There were fresh rolls and cold meats. I felt as though I was at home, these people were so fantastic. After helping with the dishes I went to sit by Gisela's side on her bed: "What is that eczema you've got, Mano?" she asked me with big eyes. "I don't have eczema," I replied. She repeated the question but it went over my head. Soon her parents appeared. I remained a while longer, said my goodbyes and came back in the afternoon equipped with a toothbrush and razor.

Franz spent the following night with me at Gisela's side. It was almost midnight when she woke up. While Franz was giving her the swab we heard a bird chirping: "As promised, the call of the tawny owl," Franz tried to make light of the situation with his sister, knowing all too well that myth associated this creature with bad luck and death. She smiled. We took it in turns to bring her the kidney dish she was so nauseous.

It was the 16th February. I found a letter from my employer in my letter box. I immediately suspected that it had to be a letter of dismissal. Evidently I had been absent from work once too often. Gisela was all that counted right now. I would find other work.

In the early afternoon there was a discernible change to Gisela's breathing. I notified her parents and her brother, who arrived at the hospital in no time. By the evening she was no longer responsive. Her mother, Franz and I remained with her. Once again it was a stormy night. Gisela slept most of the time. At seven in the morning I was so tired that I finally managed to catch some sleep. Afterwards when I was having breakfast my eye inadvertently caught the date on the calendar. *17ᵗʰ February*. Exactly seven years ago today! In my mind's eye I could see Gisela waiting at the flower vendor at Cologne Central Station – the scene was so vivid as though it were yesterday.

Gisela's father came by in the course of the morning. We ate lunch together in the kitchen. After I had washed the dishes with Sister Lydia I went back to Gisela. Her mother left the room to find comfort from her husband. Every so often Gisela's breathing faltered and I would get a fright. Sister Lydia came by. The look in her eyes said everything, silently answering the unspoken question on my lips. I stroked Gisela's hand and face.

She began gasping for air the very moment that her mother came back into the room. Then abruptly her breathing stopped. It was incomprehensible to me that she was no longer breathing. Gisela had passed on.

My mother-in-law left the room crying. "I was there for her first breath, now I am here for her last breath," she uttered in bewilderment. Her brother wasn't there, he had gone home a little earlier to sort out a few things.

Now I was alone with Gisela in the room. I was looking into her face when I suddenly felt a presence with us in the room. Was it her soul, which had left the body? It seemed to be just below the ceiling. The *entity* came across as an oversized bodily organ. In that very moment it became as clear as daylight to me that death is not the end of everything. Our soul lives on for all eternity. Gisela had passed in a state of love and dignity. I bid her farewell and left the room. In the passage I cried my eyes out with Sister Lydia comforting me. While her parents and Franz, who had meanwhile come back, and his wife Anne said their final farewells, I went to sit in the kitchen staring out of a window.

The nurses had dressed Gisela and asked me if I wanted to see her one more time. They had placed the white orchids in her folded hands. I gave my darling a kiss and wished her well on her journey. Afterwards, all I wanted was to be alone. I went outside to the car park, paced up and down in my slippers and thin jumper. It began to snow lightly. I felt empty inside. I could not think straight. At some point in time I felt the biting cold on my skin; I went back inside the hospital in a daze, sank into one of the black armchairs in the entrance hall. Franz appeared after a while, tried to impress upon me that I needed to let family and friends know. Seeing the state I was in, he volunteered the task that was evidently impossible for me at that point.

Franz and Anne urged me to spend the night at their home. I just wanted peace and quiet and to be alone, I just wanted to get home as fast as I could. In the evening I garnered up the strength to phone my parents and some friends. Afterwards I lay on top of the bed. I stared into the darkness through the open window. Not a breath of fresh air. No movement.

Absolute silence! A silence only broken by the call of the tawny owl. It felt as though Gisela was saying goodbye one last time. The gesture moved my heart deeply.

"I miss you my darling, I love you and will love you my whole life," were the words that came to my lips and which I sent into the night.

13 The wise in heart

That Sunday morning my world felt as though it had been turned completely upside down, surreal and unreal. *What now? How am I supposed to carry on? She had stopped breathing from one second to the next.* I felt alone and tired. On Rainer's recommendation I had been taking sedatives in the past few days.

There were an inordinate number of things to arrange in the days that followed: The death notice, the funeral, all kinds of formalities and administrative matters with the authorities. Franz and Anne were a huge help, lending a hand wherever they could. On the wishes of Gisela's parents, the following announcement of her death was sent to Cologne's largest daily newspaper,

> *The wise in heart*
> *mourn not for those that live,*
> *nor those that die.*
> *Every living thing lives in the life undying!*
> *The body is only a house for the spirit.*
> *Fragile, in death it shall pass away.*
> *The spirit is eternal, that which is can never cease to be.*
>   *Bhagavad Gita,*

> *Our beloved Gisela is to be laid to rest at a later stage on the island of Bali.*

On the way back home from the funeral parlour I started thinking about the eulogy at Gisela's funeral. Daniel, our friend and former neighbour who had left such beautiful messages on the door of our apartment for Gisela, immediately came to mind .The undertaker had recommended a local priest, but Gisela would not want that, I was certain of this. I phoned Daniel that evening. He and his wife Sandra assured me that I could depend on them to deliver Gisela's eulogy.

True to what Gisela had wished for her funeral, nobody wore black. The funeral parlour had decorated the hall with white lilies. The cremation had taken place a few days earlier in Cologne. The brown casket took its pride of place on the altar adorned with flowers. There were so many people who had turned up.

Daniel and Sandra began to read the eulogy:
We read on Gisela's card:
"The wise in heart
mourn not for those that live,
nor those that die.
Every living thing lives in the life undying!
The body is only a house for the spirit.
Fragile, in death it shall pass away.
The spirit is eternal, that which is can never cease to be."

That is what the enlightening Indian verse from the Bhagavad-Gita, a section of the sixth book of the Mahabharata — the song of the sublime - says.

It says: "Mourn not for those that live," yet we are gathering here today for a funeral. Grief is almost superhuman, an eternal farewell from the familiar. We need grief to draw new strength. Gisela would most certainly not have found fault with our sorrow, but she would certainly have held on to the hope that we would be confident in the fact that we have not lost her. "The spirit is eternal, that which is can never cease to be." This is also the spirit in which her plea to us, not to wear funeral garb on this day, is to be understood.

We can only talk about Gisela from the perspective from which we got to know her. Yet we are sure, that all of us will pay tribute to her memory in their own way.

Gisela's knew both life's highs and lows, sorrows and joy, togetherness and separation. Today we ask ourselves: What was it that made Gisela special as a person?

She lived this life in her own quiet way, without cues from the drum roll, without a blinding façade, without false pride, always in peace and harmony.

What was the mark that Gisela left on life?
That there is a need for harmony, the need to be young at heart both on the inside and outside.
Silent endurance was hers, always a calming force, she always had a listening ear.

At times with sadness but mostly joyful,
often pensive, always loyal.

She would listen to you, never to boast,
just when your heart needed it the most.

She so loved all things fine,
the sunshine, good food and wine...

But life also took its toll.
Tough at times, not on a roll.
A path that taught her to live in the now, not obsess in the past,
to live every day, exuberant and alive, as though it were her last.

Sometimes a familiar fragrance in the air
would entice her to places beyond compare.
When a hint from yesterday
would unexpectedly show her the way
to a new and exciting life goal,
only her Bali could fulfil that role.

The island of Bali, the island of the Gods, the western-most of the Lesser Sunda Islands in Indonesia, became the destination of their travels over and over again for Gisela and Mano.

Smells, fragrances and the wind were an integral part of Gisela's life. Her senses were so acute that she even believed she could still smell Bali though thousands of kilometres away. Bali became part of her core, internalising it as her second home:

Since time immemorial Bali has been home to a peaceful tolerant people, who live in carefree harmony with its abundant environment. A lively peace-loving tolerant nation that has a keen spiritual awareness; is artistically gifted, with life playing itself out in harmony with the gods and with divine homage to theme permeating their everyday existence! A life in which nature and fate are closely synchronised, so much so that the best send-off the dead can be given as they set out on their journey into the afterlife, is that they may be granted an earthly re-birth on the trusted island.

No doubt it will bring a smile to the faces of all who remembered Gisela's conviction that she would one day be reborn on the island of Bali and call the place home? For the sceptics, in case there are any among you, re-birth from a Balinese perspective is possible only after a considerable period of time has elapsed. First the previous life has to be processed to gain an understanding of its purpose. Re-birth is the strife towards something not accomplished in the previous life, in other words it means you can improve yourself further — until such time as your existence has reached perfection.

Especially Gisela and Mano, and of course also Gisela's parents, brother, friends, relations and work colleagues long held up hope, together with the doctors and nurses, that they could conquer the illness; an illness characterised by protracted malignancy, which once at an advanced stage holds out little chance of recovery. Even so: On the outside Gisela remained hopeful for a long time.

Gisela leaves her earthly existence at the age of 41. We experience this as very soon, much too soon. Even though it was not a sudden death, even though — as per Gisela's wish — we should not be mourning her. We are all in deep pain at her death nonetheless.

The biblical preacher and teacher of wisdom says in the book of Ecclesiastics: "I have come to the realisation: The only thing the human being can do for his own happiness is to enjoy life as long as it is ours to enjoy."

We believe Gisela lived a long life in her own right, has lived life more fully than people living to a ripe old age. In the end: Having lived this life in the entirety of its uniqueness — despite the highs and lows, despite the fight and rebellion against the illness and despite the incomprehension as to "Why me?" — to Gisela this meant having found her inner peace. "Having sorted out everything" meant already having reached a new, higher order here on earth. Which means that already in dying there is new life: Gisela's death holds a new life.

The man who nurtured the strong young eagle back to health and freedom had this to say when he set the bird free: "He will come back again, I believe he will come back again, I know for certainty he will come back again, but if he is to return, then he must first be allowed to leave."

The handkerchiefs had come out long before the end of the eulogy. As Daniel delivered the last sentence the strains of Gisela's favourite music could be heard echoing from the loudspeakers.

During the wake at a nearby restaurant afterwards, Rainer told me that even with radiation or chemo Gisela would not have stood a chance of survival with the aggressive illness. She had made the right decision not to have to endure the strain of these therapies. Patients, who undergo them, go through so much, I think to myself. What a blessing for those who make it back to life

I drove back to the hospice a few days after the funeral with a bunch of flowers a gesture of thanks for Sister Lydia from the palliative ward. I had already written hospital management a short letter expressing my sincere gratitude for the admirable work the doctors, nurses, interns and volunteers were performing.

Sister Lydia welcomed me and we went for cup of coffee, her words of comfort and support meant so much. Gisela had spent almost five weeks in the Hospice. They were the last weeks of her life. The people working there had contributed enormously towards her being able to spend this time in tranquillity and peace and with dignity. Before I said my farewells, I went to see the woman with whom Gisela had shared a room for a while. She was ever so pleased to see me. She told me her conversations with me about dying and death had been a huge help for her. She could not broach topics like that with her husband. All he would say is: "Death is death, don't talk to me about it." I could empathise with her husband. It is the hardest thing in the world to see a partner, child, parent or friend suffering and having to say goodbye to them.

At the beginning of March the following fax arrived for Franz from Bali:

Consul General W. Frenzen
Honorary Consul of the Federal Republic of Germany for Bali, USA Tenggara Barat (NTB)
Indonesia

Dear Mr
Franz Gerhard   *Sanur, the 28th February 1996*

Re.: Request for Assistance, your fax from 26th February 1996

Dear Mr Gerhard,

We hereby advise you that we have taken receipt of your fax from 26th February 1996.

A final resting place for the ashes of your deceased sister is only possible through a local funeral company. On Bali the following company would be responsible for offering the service:
Biro Jasa "Antar Bangsa"

Funeral Service
Mr Gus Sumastra
Jalan Raya Legian 384
Kuta Denpasar, Bali

Mr Gus Sumastra would collect the casket with the ashes that must be sent as cargo from the airport and provide all the necessary documentation and authorisations. He will additionally arrange for laying the ashes to rest.

Releasing the ashes into a river is not possible due to Balinese custom. The ashes can only be released into the ocean. In the event that you require further assistance please do not hesitate to contact us once more.

Yours sincerely

It had been Gisela's express wish to be laid to rest at the waterfall at GitGit. How could I possibly not honour her last wish? It was inconceivable to me.

14 Letting go

I was devastated by Gisela's death; while she was still breathing I was strong for her. When she was gone I felt so helpless, sad and alone. My friend Rainer tried to help, he prescribed tranquilisers, but I was still in a terrible state. Rainer sent me to a psychiatrist who had me hospitalised immediately. Rainer told me afterwards that he had been terribly worried about me.

I spent four weeks in a sanatorium. I can't remember a lot about that period, my overwhelming memory is of relief at not being so desperately alone. Therapy helped me, I felt in safe hands, and it was good that there were other patients that I could talk with, who understood my loss.

Slowly I got some of my power back. I needed to if I was going to accompany Franz to Bali to lay Gisela's ashes to rest. In mid-April I was allowed back home to the apartment, three weeks later Franz and I left for Bali. On my return from Bali a feeling of coldness and emptiness permeated every part of my life. The flat had become like a shrine to Gisela there were so many mementos that were a constant reminder of her. Her stylish red winter coat, the pièce de résistance of her wardrobe which she adored, still had its pride of place among her things. It was hanging there as if waiting for her.

I hardly had any contact to my fellow human beings especially during the week. I did not go out at all, completely withdrew into my own world. It was not a good thing. Weekends spent with Markus interspersed by visits from my parents, conversations with Ramona and with my brother made for the little variety my world had been relegated to. Claudia, my sister-in-law and good friend, because of her demanding job that had her work long hours, could not see me as often as I would have liked. When the opportunity did present itself, we would talk on the phone sometimes an hour at a time. They were conversations that revived me with renewed strength and courage.

I was frustrated, looked for a job but to no avail. I so badly needed the distraction. Grief had me in its powerful grip. Then somewhere out of nowhere the idea came to me to write a book about what I was going through. On some days I would write until the early hours. I would go for long walks in between to re-energise and clear my head to get new perspectives.

Somehow the days past. I made good progress with my writing. Writing, I discovered, gave me peace although I would often also find myself crying inconsolably as I relived so many of the key moments of the past seven years. Writing forced me to go through a devastating roller coaster of emotions.

In the autumn I finally plucked up the courage, and packed all Gisela's clothes – including her red coat – into eight large bags to donate to the Red Cross. By December the book was ready. I could not be any prouder of myself. I was certain that I had created something invaluable and inherently knew that it had likewise been Gisela's unspoken wish to spread her story around the world so as to be a help to others. More importantly, to give people hope! Even if the book were to help only one person, it would have been worth the effort.

Simply the thought of Christmas made me sad. Markus came to stay with me for a few days. Having to entertain a ten year old, occupied me. Markus's company was and is always a source of comfort to me. He of course was also grieving the death of Gisela, as was Ramona, they had both been good friends of hers.

The New Year was around the corner, I was determined to find a job. I placed five adverts in different dailies. Unfortunately, again to no avail. I was depressed, especially since gainful employment would have been of great benefit to me not only from a financial point of view, but for many other reasons as well. The winter was upon us, the grey days did little to lift my spirits. I had to make a change, but did not know where to begin. I thought about our holiday in Gran Canaria and reached for my travel guide on La Palma in the bookshelf. The book describes the island as strikingly green. Without giving it a second thought I headed off to the closest travel agent and enquired about package tours. Despite the agent's best efforts, none of the package tours on offer seemed to strike a chord with me, they were not what I had in mind. Before I knew it I had simply booked myself a return flight to the island. The trip was beginning to fall into place in an effortless, unhurried manner. As though it was meant to be! As if by divine intervention! If anything, this was a sign for me that it was the right decision. Life had taught me that when you try to force things into a certain direction, when your intentions feel heavy with resistance, the time is not right or that road ahead is not meant to be.

It was mid-January when I headed to Düsseldorf Airport, a large suitcase in tow. The mercury was hovering at four degrees. It was cold and wet outside, drizzling slightly. I was happy when the plane took off. Four hours later La Palma bid me welcome. It was overcast, yet pleasantly warm at 20 degrees Celsius. At that moment in time I intrinsically knew that this had been the right decision. My holiday accommodation in Puerto Naos was in the west of La Palma. It had once been a small fishing village. I had read in my travel guide that the west of the island boasted an annual average of 3300 hours of sunshine. In contrast to the sun-kissed west the east of the island could find itself draped in clouds for most of the winter.

From the outset La Palma was kind to me. Outside the airport building I became acquainted with an elderly couple busy loading their luggage into their rental car. Since they were also heading to the west of the island they offered me a ride as far Los Llanos. Simply the drive in itself already brought home to me the beauty of the green island. A highlight was driving through the tunnel that connected the east with the west. In Los Llanos I took a bus to Puerto Naos. En route I got chatting to a young couple who advised me of a place that rented out holiday accommodation. I had had misgivings about my foreign language skills before the trip, so in some ways surprised even myself at how effortless booking a four-week holiday apartment was in the end.

It soon became clear to me that this trip was precisely what I needed. It helped me gain a new perspective on my life and the warming effect of the sun somehow gave me a more optimistic outlook on the future. I began exploring the island with a rental car, its diverse beauty never ceasing to amaze me. At the Orinoco, a restaurant in Puerto Naos, I had the good fortune to meet Rainer and Arno, two guys from Düsseldorf only a 45 minute drive from Cologne where I lived. Its great prices and good food meant that I found myself wiling away the time there on most evenings. True to its name, "a navigable place" the Orinoco was a place people would pass through with ease, it was a place that had a tendency to bring like-minded individuals together.

Renate and Bodo from Lüneburg in the so-called North German Plains were two such like-minded individuals the Orinoco had brought into my life. It was at time when the anniversary of Gisela's death was just around the corner. I was already dreading the day. Renate and Bodo were like a godsend, they took me with them to El Remo, a small village by the sea, for the day. Even if they may not have been aware of it, their company and the conversations we had were wonderful food for the soul. I could not be more grateful for not having to spend the day alone.

Unbeknown to me as yet, La Palma was to give me something that would become a pivotal point in my life. I woke up with a start the one morning, the dream that I had torn myself from still as clear as daylight: Gisela's body lay on a gurney. At each corner there stood a man. There were four men in all. At the foot of the stretcher I could clearly read her name: *Gisela Gerhard-*. Our surname *Link* was missing. Her full name after we got married was *Gisela Gerhard-Link*. The dream unsettled me. It had me preoccupied all day.

After sunset on the beach I had a chance to talk about the dream with Marion, a woman I had met from Switzerland. Even as we were speaking I began to grasp the message the dream held for me: I had to let go. All too often I was still holding 'dialogues' with Gisela, venting about my suffering and lamenting my heartache. I had only been a part of her life. Grace had let me live at her side for exactly seven years.

Marion gave me some well-meant advice: "Let Gisela go! Set her free. You'll soon feel better. Our partners, children and friends are not our possessions. I too have lost friends to death and have had to release them. After all if I think about it, they continue to live inside me. Their love, their expressions, their words, their laughter and tears continue to remain within my being. What is more, they have already taken a part of me with them. My words, my love – everything they received from me. They took it with them to a new life, to another world, their new world."

My gaze followed the sun slowly sinking into the Atlantic Ocean, Marion's words swept away by the waves, which gently deposited their foamy crowns on the black sand. Yes, I thought. I have to let go. "Find a special place," Marion went on. "A church or somewhere in nature, pray for Gisela and in the silence tell her that you are setting her free."

The very next morning I rented myself a car and drove to the north of La Palma. In Don Pedro, an idyllic village in the midst of dreamy nature I parked the car and began walking aimlessly past its houses my sights set on the deep blue ocean all the while. A wooden cross on a small rise caught my attention. In that instance it became as clear to me as daylight that there was no place on earth more suited to what I needed to do. I climbed up to the cross and stood before it. A light warm breath of wind wrapped itself around me, as though it wanted to take me in. I felt protected, as though I were in a cocoon. The words came to my lips, silently. I knew exactly what I was going to say without having to give it even a second thought. The words came from afar: "Dear Gisela, I thank you for the love you have bestowed upon me. Your friendship, the life with you and that I could learn from you and grow with you. I will always love you and will no longer burden you with my heartbreak and suffering. I am setting you free."

Then slowly I made my way past the cacti that lined the path and headed back down the hill, staring at the ocean deep in thought. Something was going on inside of me, gently and lovingly processing what had transpired only moments earlier. Before I got into the car I turned around one more time, looked up at the cross. A powerful sense of peace overcame me. On the drive back it became infinitely clear to me how important it was to let go. Letting go meant setting the scene for a new life. Letting go also meant taking responsibility for oneself and one's life. It takes time, courage and strength – most of all it takes love.

It was the second-last day of my holiday in La Palma. As usual I was enjoying my breakfast sitting on my balcony. The thought of having to leave the island did not resonate well with me. I had meanwhile become friends with a number of visitors and people who lived here. The climate was good for me and I liked being in nature. Saying goodbye was hard.

15 A new lease on life

I arrived at Düsseldorf Airport. I would have given anything to get on the next flight back to La Palma everything felt so cold. To add insult to injury I missed my train by literally seconds. My mood levels had been dropping during the flight to Germany. On a feel-good scale of one to ten, they had now reached rock bottom. There were so many thoughts racing through my head: Work, everyday life in Leverkusen. How would I be able to go on with it all? I was alone, it was dismal and cold, winter was still here... relentless.

In the months that followed I struggled to build a new life for myself, somehow I was failing at it miserably. I felt depressed and weary of life. It felt as though I had already lived an entire lifetime. What else was there to wish for? Could I still experience more and even if so, did I really want to? What was left here for me anyway? My parents, my children, my brother as well as a circle of friends that I could probably count on one hand. I'm not good at asking for help. It was rare in my life for me to seek help from anyone. Since childhood I had learnt to deal with my own problems.

Now in my state of utter desperation I had decided to turn to God as a last resort "Dear God," I prayed. "Please show me the way to happiness once more or take me with you. From this moment on I'm going to stop making wishes and cease my unrealistic expectations. You know what is best for me. You are far greater than I am." It was with these words that I placed my life in God's hands. I did not have even the slightest notion that this prayer would steer my life into a direction that I did not deem possible even in my wildest dreams. A path that would be way beyond what I could ever have wished for or even thought to be vaguely possible.

God helped me in so many different ways. The few friends I did have, meant the world to my survival. Without them I would in all likelihood never have gotten back on to my feet again. A new friend, Conni had a way of showing me how to find my way out of depression. It was also she who introduced me to books about God and belief. Many hours were spent reading the spiritual literature. I engaged in philosophy and psychology, my own life always the focal point of what I read. I was growing in the process, recognising my mistakes, somehow finding renewed strength and with it succeeding in trusting my life once again. I was gradually discovering the small joys of life like yoga, meditation, cooking, going for long walks in nature, the trees and the flowers. My children helped in rediscovering joy. Markus, who lived with his mother came to stay every second weekend and we got on well together, when he was with me we would often meet Ramona.

I eventually found a job, working in administration in a big firm. It felt good to have a place to go every day and a bit more financial freedom. I felt the lack of romantic love in my life deeply – I felt very alone but any attempt at starting a new relationship was scuttled from the outset. I had come to the harsh realisation that grief and love for someone new represented conflicting interests. In the end I opted for being alone and remained single.

Every so often I returned to the book I had written after Gisela's death. I would edit and rewrite it, each time reliving the experiences. I even sent it to a few German publishers with no success. The time wasn't yet right, the story's end couldn't yet be written.

The years passed, in 2000, four years after Gisela had died I left behind our flat once and for all, and moved eighty kilometres to the beautiful green town of Bad Neuenahr in the Ahr Valley, a tributary of the River Rhine. The move meant a new beginning. Fortunately I came by a reasonably priced flat and a job. In Bad Neuenahr, Uschi came into my life. She was a very wise and older woman with whom I became very good friends. Uschi helped to guide me back into the world of the living, back to a happy, fulfilling and purpose-driven life. I would often join her on hikes in nature, far away from any cities, where most importantly there was time to talk. I always felt that Uschi was sent to help me to change my life.

The rest of my life transformation would come about thanks to the newspaper 'The Rhine Newspaper'. I still have the article that caught my attention to this day. It was dated the 17th March 2004, it was written by a certain Friedhelm Link from the town of Bad Breisig and would send a chill down my spine, unleashing some very intense feelings in my inner world. Not only did the writer live within half-an-hour drive by car from where I lived, but he *coincidentally* shared the same surname as mine. I tore out the article and put it in safekeeping for later on. The article was about the Camino de Santiago de Compostela, the old pilgrim walking route across the north of Spain. The Camino was beckoning to me but for various reasons I didn't understand fully, it would not be my destiny for another year. Life had taught me that if the time was not right, for whatever reason, then it was best to wait.

I knew little about the Camino, it was a leap into the unknown. I took little notice of Conni's words to me "You'll be coming back in October, but only to give in your notice for the flat."

It was the 28th April 2005 when in the bustling French market town of Saint-Jean-pied-de-Port at the foothills of the Pyrenees fate would make its grand entry. It was on that day that an Irish woman would set off on her pilgrimage on the Camino de Santiago de Compostela. *Coincidentally* it was on that auspicious day that I too set off on mine from the very same town. It would take all of 42 days for Jean and my first encounter in Finisterre in Galicia in north-western Spain – once considered the end of the world. Meeting one another was all the more unusual given the many factors and occurrences, in fact an inordinate number of them, that first had to play themselves out in order for our paths to cross. By then we had inadvertently formed the same friendships on our 900-kilometer walk and when we compared our pilgrimage passes afterwards we realised in retrospect that on some days we had slept over in the same village and that I had even passed Jean on one occasion, a day when relentless rain had been the order of the day, without either of us having realised it.

I had already spent a week in Finisterre, had a good time and was about to move on when a deep-seated sensation told me to wait just one more day. In the end I waited! That is how I met Jean. Hansi, another 'pilgrim' had become a friend to both me and to Jean separately. It was he who coaxed the final building blocks into place by ensuring that Jean would be at dinner with him and me that evening. After the generous meal that we were served as a gift from the family-run Hotel Ancora, the three of us went to explore the mystical place in the hills nearby where a seventh century hermit San Guillermo had once lived. We ended this magical evening on which Jean had been brought into my life by taking in the harbour lights at night.

The events that had transpired leading up to that moment when we first met could hardly be ascribed to chance. Divine intervention had to have taken place. Jean and I stayed on for three more days. Santiago de Compostela was the pilgrimage finish and it was here that with heavy hearts and tears in our eyes, the time had come to say our farewells. I had no idea what was happening to me. Overwhelmingly huge waves of emotion had come flooding into my life. My trip back home was as if in a trance. It was as though I was returning to a world that I no longer wanted, no longer liked, a world that seemed unreal to me, wrapped in a haze. My flat in Bad Neuenahr felt strange when I stepped inside. This was no longer my world. My world had changed. I had changed.

One name kept popping into my mind or should I say my world of feelings: Jean! What was this empathetic beautiful Irish woman doing to me? I began to ask myself the meaning of the feelings I was having for her. Could it be love? It was hard to pinpoint them. My limited command of English quickly had me abandon the idea of trying to phone her in Ireland. I simply could not pluck up the courage. Hansi then came to the rescue, took on the role of translator. We figured that sending texts was our best bet, this gave me enough time to have the words I was not familiar with translated and at the same time I was learning the language.

Four days after arriving back home a parcel from Ireland had arrived for me. Even before I had managed to get through the packaging to the content, my kitchen table was covered in the tiniest of silver angels that had trickled from the parcel. Jean's four-page letter accompanying the parcel unleashed some very strong emotions in me, which was a good thing because with them also came the answers to my many questions. Yes, there was no doubt about it. I had developed some very strong feelings for Jean. They were feelings of love. An angel from Clonmacnoise, a mystical town on the River

Shannon, essential oils and a music CD completed the unusual collection of gifts. They all unmistakably spoke of love. While I was listening to the music I began to cry uncontrollably. I could feel Jean's presence in the music; I kept playing it over and over again in the days to come.

We wanted to see one another again! Simply had to see one another again! Three weeks after we had said our farewells in Santiago I was waiting for her at Cologne Airport. The connection that we already had in Spain was immediately reignited, she felt so familiar to me, as though we had been together a lifetime. My English had improved a bit, I had spent as much time as I could studying it. Despite our lack of fluency in a common language communication was not a problem. We spent four wonderful and carefree days in Bad Neuenahr and we both sensed that there was far more keeping us together than a pilgrimage romance.

Before Jean made her way back to Dublin she came with me to book me a return flight to Ireland for a week later. Given the anticipation, saying goodbye was not as hard this time. Back at Cologne Airport on the 10th July, this time waiting for my flight to board, this is what I wrote in my diary: *I have a feeling that I have finally arrived. I have the distinct feeling that after 50 years of having to overcome deserts, mountains and oceans I am going home. Jean's hands are my home, her face is my home, her hair and our love is my home.*

After a one-and-a-half hour flight Ireland greeted me with glorious sunshine interspersed with light clouds. Seeing this green island country from the air for the first time stirred something inside my heart and from its depths I implicitly knew that I had arrived... at home! After passport control I waited impatiently for my suitcase then made my way to the exit, I could not help running. The glass doors opened automatically. Before me was the beaming face of my Irish angel. We held one another for a long time.

During the days that followed Jean showed me her world, her life: Ireland. She gradually introduced me to her wonderful family and friends. I cancelled my return flight on the 10th August and flew back to Germany together with Jean in mid-October, terminated my lease in as little as three days and even managed to find a new tenant. After everything was done, I remembered what Conni had said to me at the end of April before I left for my pilgrimage: *You'll be coming back in October, but only to give in your notice for the flat."* Jean got to know my family and my friends, who all took to her immediately. A week later we were back in Ireland.

Fortunately there was work for me to do in Ireland. I was busy writing a second book, this time about my pilgrimage and the transformation it had brought to my life. I would attend the language school courses regularly so as to improve my English, which was imperative to my survival in a foreign country. Ramona my daughter had meanwhile gotten married and Markus my son was living with his girlfriend Petra in Frechen, his place of birth. I was a free agent once more and with nothing holding me back any longer was ready to begin a new life in Ireland.

16 Return

Five years after I met Jean we found ourselves en route to Dublin Airport. Joyous in anticipation we sat in the back seat of the taxi holding hands. Our flight to Bali was with Singapore Airlines via London with a stopover in Singapore.

Several months earlier Jean had told me how badly she needed to get away on a holiday of sheer relaxation. She had been working hard. Far too hard in my opinion! The stresses of work had begun to leave their tell-tale signs. Her body was sending out warning signals, as the body tends to do under the strain of overwork. *Bali!* That was the destination she had come up with when I asked her where she wanted to spend her holiday. Bali! For me mere mention of the place would trigger some very powerful feelings and all I could see in my mind's eye were images of Gisela and the waterfall at GitGit. Fourteen years had gone by since I had laid Gisela to rest there in May 1996. Twice seven years − again the number: Seven. Seven has always been a special number for me, and this was confirmed by a numerology expert I met at one stage years ago.

Ever since it had become clear to me that I was destined to return to Bali, Gisela and the waterfall were foremost in my mind. I was nervous and did not have the courage to contemplate visiting GitGit in the first few days. This was going to be a special visit and I needed to be ready for it. Jean was of the opinion that I must listen to my gut feel. It would tell me when the day was right.

For the first week we were booked into a quiet hotel in the north of Bali that we both fell in love with the moment we laid eyes on it. Even though relaxation and plenty of rest were top of Jean's list of priorities, she had the kind of curiosity that would not let her miss out if an opportunity of a special kind presented itself.

Marianne, a hotel guest from the Netherlands, was someone we took to from the very first moment, she was an extremely likeable person with whom we were able to have good and meaningful conversations. One evening she suggested an outing to a special temple festival happening the next day. It was an irresistible idea. The next day we met Gede our driver and guide outside the hotel. Before we set off Gede had adeptly wrapped a colourful sarong around each of our waists and handed me a head covering, otherwise as he explained, we would have been denied access to the temple. Gede was one of these people one could immediately take a liking to. In tune with the friendly nature of the Balinese that had already become par for the course for us, he was no exception. We later learned that he was a history and English teacher and that his family hailed from the village of Les, where the temple celebrations were taking place.

The closer we got to the temple, the more believers in festive garb we came across. They were predominantly on motorbikes. Gede parked the car a few hundred metres from the temple surrounded by palm trees and the mountains. We got out and made our way uphill past a few small shops. Excited I would greet the locals we came across, I loved their smiles and reciprocating the friendliness they bestowed on me came easily to me.

Slowly we climbed the numerous steps up to the temple. I was in total awe. The harmonious atmosphere of the site had me captivated. I felt that I belonged here. I was not a Hindu, nor Catholic – the dominant faith of the Rhine region where I come from. Neither was I Buddhist nor Muslim. Still, I believe in God. I believe that God is there for everybody. Not only for Hindus, Muslims, Buddhists or people belonging to whatsoever denomination. God loves humanity and this is proof enough that he is there for everybody. What would compel a loving God to have favourites, loving a Hindu more than say a Buddhist, Muslim, Jew or Christian?

As we entered the temple, the faithful inside could not help staring at us curiously. Except for the three of us there was not another tourist in sight. Wherever I looked there was a pair of eyes smiling at me with open curiosity. We found a seat on a low wall and before we knew it were totally engrossed in the dances that were centuries old and were being re-enacted on this day. Many people greeted Gede, not surprisingly as this was his home village. Soon we also found ourselves engaged in conversation with some of the people who evidently wanted to show off their English skills.

Next we were being swept along the stream of people patiently making their way to the prayer precinct. Remembering to remove our shoes, we found ourselves a spot among the many believers. A religious song sounded from the PA system accompanied by a Gamelan orchestra. Right in front of us a young girl who could be no older than three years was gyrating to the rhythms. I looked over to Jean and Marianne. Their expressions said it all. They too had succumbed to the fascination of the festival.

A priest poured holy water into each individual's right hands held cupped. He did this three times over and following the example of Gede we then drank the water. The fourth offering of water the priest came with was intended for us to bless our heads. Following that we were given some rice grains. They had to be stuck to the forehead as part of the religious ritual. The priest handed Gede his microphone. Gede then opened a small book and he broke into religious song. The small 'princess' was dancing to the strains of the music as if in trance. I felt a deep sense of gratitude for having been brought to this place.

After the blessing, the faithful stood up, got back into their shoes and made their way to a table that seemed to go on forever. Here they placed their offerings. Gede had told us beforehand that we could make a small cash donation as an offering. After our tribute we entered our names in the guest book laid out for all to sign. Making our way past the many worshippers, we then left the prayer site to get to the forecourt where more dances were being performed. An hour later we reluctantly had to leave and go back to the hotel. As we made our way out of the temple complex, a throng of people was still coming towards us up the steps. Overcome by a deep sense of joy I used every opportunity to reach out my hands to the children in the crowd who were accompanied by their parents. Jean shook her head. Her face the picture of contentment. She knew how much the people here meant to me and especially the children. She knew me well. How much it meant to me to approach people to show them that I cared and that they mattered.

"We automatically get on well," was Gede's answer to my question as to why children in Bali do not cry or scream much and on the whole tend to behave themselves, are never loud or obnoxious. He explained to us that right from the start Balinese children are lovingly accepted into the family and into the village community and protected accordingly. From a very early age they learn the art of everyday life: How to prepare food and offerings and the rituals which pay tribute to the Gods. It gives them a structure that is important to their lives and that of their fellow human beings. The family's love gives them strength, self-confidence and most of all a sense of self-worth which many children in the western world today are lacking. I have always felt the high rates of depression, hopelessness and illness among young people in the western world are greatly contributed to by the absence of familial love that surrounds the Balinese.

I gave the fact that the Balinese are more relaxed, satisfied and happier than us Europeans a lot of thought. The more I pondered on this phenomenon the more apparent it was to me that it had to do with their belief system, their lifestyle and the congenial circumstances of their childhood environment. Why do people surrounded by love flourish better, thrive? Could it be that it is because they themselves in essence are love and believe this. Moreover they are showered with love from their parents, grandparents and the community as a whole that they live in. Of course they are not perfect. They too have their weaknesses, a shadow side. Yet it is *how* they deal with this shadow side and their demons, that makes the difference. Not only do they pay homage to the Gods, they also make offerings to the evil forces to appease them. The Balinese believe that to deny their existence would be a disservice to truth. This, I thought to myself, is utterly extraordinary. If a person recognises his or her dark side, if he acknowledges it, he is more likely to be able to disperse it in love and light. If however this side is not known to a person, these forces can continue to torment him or her in way that could cause them and those around them great unhappiness, because they are not aware of what it is that is that is tormenting them.

Much of the drive back to the hotel I was in a contemplative mood thinking about Bali and its people. The Balinese bless just about everything in their lives, be it the fruit and vegetables they eat, the flowers that adorn their surroundings, the garments they wear or the spices they add to their food. Two days later on our visit to the market we discovered they also blessed their market stalls and all the food that is to be sold. I think it can be said without any fear of contradiction that they bless everything. It is this act of blessing all, and accepting these blessings that makes everything in Bali so special. What could be better than partaking of food that has been blessed? What better way to eat than at a restaurant that is blessed several times a day? We in the Western World could live together a bit more joyfully and harmoniously if we were to bestow blessings on one another as the Balinese do. We reached our hotel and said goodbye to Gede, thanked him profusely, telling him that we felt abundantly gifted by the events of the day.

That evening I sat on the patio in front of our bungalow and looked across the vast expanse of ocean. Jean was relaxing by the pool. My thoughts drifted away with the gentle warm breeze and re-emerged in a world that was strange and new to me. I felt the love and harmony of Bali, I could sense and feel its revelation to me – the messages it held for me. On entering this world I let go of my own thoughts, they dissipated in the love, in the eternity embraced by my soul. I felt true happiness. It was as if my soul yearned to return to the lap of eternal love, pure love, to God – the origin of all things, the source – the definitive core of where we come from.

Letting go – I must keep reminding myself that I must let go and trust in my path. Surely there was nothing that warranted greater trust than my God-given destiny? For a long time I had ceased to believe in what people described as *coincidence*. There exists a guided tour unique to each one of us. A tour where we were always in the place we were meant to be, where the things that happened to us were meant to happen to us. If only we would have more trust this would take us to where we ought to be to fulfil our unique life plan. It is not always easy, sometimes tumultuous events shake us to the core; yes, even then we are looked after and given help. The purpose of our life can be gleaned from life itself. The purpose of life *is* life.

It is as if Bali exists to remind us what we could create with our world if we would have more trust and live more fully. Here the people live serenely drawing on an intrinsic understanding deep within their hearts that all is okay; Living every moment with an appreciation of the beauty and blessings that surround us all.

As I sat there I prayed *Bali – Hold me close, give me solace and protect me from my fears. Hold me in your love. I thank you for the wealth of gifts your tropical realm has bestowed upon me. Bali – island of the Gods – you have gifted me like no other, caressing me with the budding revitalising life force that is yours and have planted infinite love in the depths of my heart. You have given me so much and are still giving: providing me with a comfort zone while sowing new seeds, encouraging me to set myself new goals to give and received back infinitely more than I could ever conceive or dream of.*

The gifts of Bali continued that evening. Marianne told us about a healer who lived quite close by in the middle of the jungle. Even if we did not have any ailments she felt we would both benefit with a visit to him. Jean had trouble with her back, so there was no question about giving this a try and we had reception make us an appointment to see the healer. I was fortunate not to have any health issues but was sure that a healing massage would do me no harm.

The very next day, we were on our way. Our driver who also doubled up as our interpreter took us through the last stretch on foot, since our destination was a house by a small stream that could only be reached by a narrow path. Jean looked at me with big eyes. Her expression spoke volumes: What on earth are we doing here in the middle of the jungle on the way to a person whom we do not know with no idea of what he might come up with? I could not help laughing. Jean began laughing with me, the laughter easing any apprehension she may have felt.

Our guide took us through the entrance, past the house temple and introduced us to the healer. From the first instant, I could see in his eyes that he had healing powers. The driver translated what the healer was telling us and while we sipped the tasty sweet tea put before us, he told us that during the treatment we should ask him questions, if we had any. While I was enjoying my tea, I was thinking about questions regarding my health then followed the healer up a few steps to a small room that was only separated by a curtain. I got undressed except for my underwear and lay on the mat on my stomach. The healer using coconut oil massaged me slowly and deeply. I could feel every rib individually. It was as though questions were being put to my organs and bones. *What is your status? Everything working as it should? Everything okay?* The issues and questions I had at the outset began clarifying themselves. I felt an energy enter my body and mind. Half way through I was motioned to sit up for my shoulders and back to get their turn, my body gratefully accepting the revitalising force. While my chest was being massaged I had the urge to look the healer in the eyes. His eyes shone, radiated spirituality and spoke of trust and healing. The messages that came to me held great clarity. The massage part of the healing over, I got dressed again, stepped outside the curtain and went back to Jean and the driver who were sitting by the table, chatting and drinking tea. I did not say a word to Jean, simply smiled at her, let the driver wrap a sarong around my hips before the healer guided me to the temple.

I felt a great sense of ease in the presence of the healer as I stood before the family temple where from a coconut shell he poured the water covered in petals into my hands. The ritual was repeated three times, with me having to drink the water afterwards each time. He then poured the remaining water over my head. I could not help smiling to myself. It reminded me of a baptism. I then followed him into a small room where I sat on a stool. He lit a match and held it under three incense sticks, which soon emitted a pleasing scent. I was a little taken aback when he placed a small dagger in my hand and motioned me to close my hand into a fist. Then the mysterious ceremony ended with him drawing a symbol on my forehead and tying a thin red and white band around my wrist, which he blessed with the incense. I then did as the driver had advised me. I put the agreed to sum of money for the treatment into the offering bowl handed to me, covered it with a palm leaf and with a bow handed it over to the healer. The healer received the bowl with a nod of his head. In closing, he invited me to sit at a small table to clarify any remaining questions. I showed the healer a dark mole that had been worrying me and asked him whether I should have it removed. He assured me it was no cause for concern. Then he looked me over one more time, gave me the thumbs up and with great conviction in his voice uttered one word: *Bagus!* What more could I want? My body and I were *bagus*. Everything was *good! Good* plain and simple. I was extremely happy about this and decided to ask the healer one more question. I was keen to know if I had healing powers to heal others. He closed his eyes but at the same time it felt that he was looking me over once more, this time with his senses. He nodded. He then showed me the approach I should take to heal others: The important thing was for my body and chakras to be pure. Beaming with joy I thanked him and left Jean in his healing hands, while I went to sit at the table with the driver.

It was some time before Jean reappeared from behind the curtain. I took one look at her and knew that the massage treatment had been beneficial for her also. Once Jean had completed the rituals that followed we said our farewells to this humble human being whose eyes spoke volumes. He truly had healing powers. There was no doubt in my mind. I asked the driver to tell him that we were both extremely happy with the session and that we wished him and his family everything of the very best. We placed both hands together, bowed our heads and embraced one another before we left his house. Back at the hotel, we let the healing effect of the day's events prolong themselves by relaxing in the sun. At dinner we thanked Marianne for having guided us to such an invaluable experience.

Bagus — I could not get enough of the word. It would become my constant companion in the weeks and months that followed. The band around my wrist was a constant reminder and a welcome one at that: I was *bagus*. Healthy! I could not contain my joy. I was endlessly grateful that I had followed my intuition, listened to my gut feel and had been able to succumb to the healing massage. There was plenty in life that I could do without. My gut feel was not one of these things. It spoke to me in unequivocal terms, always giving me the answers. In retrospect I count my lucky stars that I have listened to it time and again and paid heed to it, allowing me to embrace all that is *bagus*, helping me to circumvent that which is not.

17 The magic of Bali at work

Today was the day!

It was the fifth morning of our stay, I woke up earlier than usual and my intuition told me that today had to be the day. I went downstairs to make the arrangements. The palm basket that I had reception organise for me contained the Frangipani blossoms that Gisela had been so fond of.

The Balinese people believe that they have an endless number of lives. I find the idea of being born and then dying after one life inconceivable. To me the idea of being reborn makes infinitely more sense than having only one life. Only one life – and that is it? I believe that we live forever and that the body decays, but that the soul is eternal. I have always hoped that I would grow old and then die happily feeling my time here is complete! You can now take me with you to heaven! I would love to die with a feeling of joyful anticipation as if I was going on a long trip. Obviously this is up to my creator!

I was long convinced that Gisela had been reborn again onto a new life in Bali. The thought that she could potentially cross my path somewhere, as a young girl or boy, had me excited beyond compare. I found the idea fascinating, and very comforting.

The car and driver to take us to GitGit arrived. Jean took hold of my hand and smiled at me. She could sense my anxiety knowing that I had gone through so much. She had been my rock time and again, her love and understanding giving me the strength to carry on. The journey by taxi was unhurried with the driver cautiously negotiating the streets of Northern Bali although they were still quiet at that time of day. Every now and again a motorbike would come hurtling towards us. Cars were few and far between. The driver estimated the trip to take approximately an hour. Gazing out of the window, I could not get enough of the sights Bali had to offer. Emerging around every corner was something interesting and new to capture the imagination, be it temples, flowers, trees, people and animals. Bali was endowed with an abundance of all things beautiful. Riches that had nothing to do with money.

GitGit had changed. Obviously 14 years would change a place and its people. I too had changed, had learnt many new things and had experienced a lot. I had two pilgrimages on the Camino de Santiago de Compostela to my name, five years living in Ireland and Galicia in north Spain. I could now speak English fluently and my command of the Spanish language had also improved. I had become more mature and had found happiness once again – Jean had been a very important part in this.

I took the palm basket with me. We slowly made our way down the winding path to the waterfall accompanied by our driver. It was a pleasant warm morning. The decision to go early was paying off. The souvenir shops were still closed and there was not a tourist in sight. Jean was delighted at the prolific vegetation, the smells, colours and the palm trees. I was glad to have her by my side. I felt that I was in the right place right here and now. When we reached the waterfall I anxiously got stuck into trying to identify the spot where we had laid Gisela's ashes to rest. This area too had become prey to the sands of time which had completely transformed it.

Jean was waiting for me at the temple near the waterfall. After a short search I was certain that I had found the spot. I motioned to Jean and she came down the path and took me in her arms. I felt moved. I laid the flowers on a big stone and said a prayer. Then I gently scattered some of the flowers onto the water. I felt sure that Gisela was happy, wherever she was. That was what my heart was telling me. The conviction underlying this message put me in a good mood. Jean released the remaining flowers into the water noticeably moved and said a silent prayer. Then we embraced one another and set off to the temple arm in arm. Jean took a few photos of me with the waterfall in the background. Weeks later our friend Hansi wrote to ask whether we had noticed that a section of the cascading water was in the shape of an angel touching my shoulder. After examining the photo over and over, the realisation once again sent a chill down our spines. The signs that Gisela and Bali were sending us were unmistakable.

It was incredibly difficult to say goodbye. Jean liked GitGit and I knew she also liked Gisela, she had told me so. Claudia was of the opinion that Gisela had played a role in having Jean and I meet. We climbed up the steps, slowly.

On one level everything that had happened in the past fourteen years seemed surreal, bizarre and inexplicable. Yet from the surreal and inexplicable it had become clear to me that around us and within us there exists another strange world, which we know and intuitively feel, but which we cannot conceive of with our logical reasoning and which we do not necessarily have to comprehend. I found this wonderful world fascinating. Looking back I felt as if I had been guided every step of the way. I felt I had been blessed with so many miracles. This wonderful world had opened its doors to me after I had opened myself to it. Entry to it is not granted unless you let it in – whatever we do not believe in cannot enter our lives. We have to be prepared to open ourselves up and we have to be prepared for miracles and wonders. Jean reached out her hand to me and brought me back down to earth. We watched the people harvesting cloves near the path back up the road. Eventually we got into the car and made our way back to the hotel. I felt at peace during the drive.

It was still only mid-morning when we arrived back at the hotel and climbed the stairs to the restaurant serving breakfast. Two smiling Balinese women welcomed us inside. We took our time over breakfast, ordering champagne in acknowledgement of such a very special day and drank a toast to Gisela.

Jean and I both knew how to enjoy life and that was a good thing. We lived life to the fullest. We were both keenly aware that it could end in a heartbeat, and all we could do was to live in the moment. Living in the moment and seeing and appreciating the love, the blessings and the miracles was the key to happiness.

Jean told me that she was glad to have been to Gisela's final resting place in GitGit. I thanked my darling that she was with me. Tears began to well up in my eyes. The waitress serving us a fresh cup of delicious coffee had become a blur. An embarrassed *terima kasih* came to my lips in acknowledgement. Jean took my hand and it was only now that I saw that she too had tears in her eyes.

The magic of Bali was at work.

Acknowledgements

My thanks to:
Gisela for her love.
My parents Katharina and Ferdinand and my brother
Heinz-Dieter.
Jean for her love and support.
My beloved children Ramona and Markus.
Sandra, Claudia

Birgitt Lederer for the excellent translation.
Regina Karolyi and Monika Thees for their valuable
editing.
Paula Nolan for designing the beautiful cover.
Karina Pfolz of Karina Verlag, Vienna, who published
the original German language edition of this book (and
awarded it first prize in 2018) and who also published
Phillippe, *Insua* and *Love Never Ends*.
Martin Urbanek and the other Karina Verlag authors
for all their help and encouragement.
Tracy Brennan of the Trace Literary Agency, USA, for
believing in this book and for all her work and support.

Lorna Byrne for her prayers and blessings.
Christopher Reburn for his enthusiasm and support.
Janet de Neefe, founder of the Ubud Writers and
Readers Festival, and all her team, for creating what in
my opinion is the best literature festival in the world.

Rüdiger Heins for his support and advice and in particular for giving me a Creative Writing scholarship at the beginning of my career.
Dr Peter Arnds of Trinity College Dublin.
My colleagues in the Irish Writers Centre, in particular the members of the nIce writing group.
The Goethe Institute Ireland for hosting two book launches.

My wonderful German support team: Angelika, Andrea and Andreas wunderbaR Konsum, Steffi and Eddy.

Finally, thanks to all my friends in Ireland who have been encouraging me to publish this book in English so as they can read it. I am grateful to Jean's extensive family, my neighbors in Vernon Street, Donal, Marc and Noel in the Iveagh Gardens, Noelle and Tom, Marie and Maurice, Rory, Breda, Kyran, Katherine, Seamus, Rita, Frau Schneider, Tim, Kate, Pearl, Aideen, Gandhi, Razan, Bas, Raneem, Serene and so many others.

About Manolo Link
Manolo Link was born in Frechen near Cologne, Germany, and now lives between there, Dublin, Ireland and Finisterre, Galicia, Spain.

Manolo has published six books: Two autobiographical works *A New Life on Bali and A New Life on the Camino* and four inspirational novels *Philippe, Maria Milena, Insua,* and *Love Never Ends.*

A New Life on Bali is his first book to be translated into English.

Manolo and his books have been featured in newspapers, magazines, radio and TV in Germany, Austria, Ireland, Spain and the USA. He has been interviewed and given readings at the Frankfurt, Leipzig and Vienna Book Fairs, and at a series of events across Ireland, Germany, Switzerland, Austria and Spain. His love of Bali has led to his participation on two occasions in the Ubud Writers and Readers Festival, an international literary festival held in Bali.

In addition to writing books, Manolo runs creative writing workshops.

For more see: www.manololink.com
Facebook: Manolo Link, Author
Twitter: @manololink

Other books by Manolo Link

This book was published in German by Karina Verlag, Vienna under the title *Ein neues Leben auf Bali*.

Karina Verlag has also published Manolo Link's books: *Liebe endet nie*, *Philippe* and *Insua*. **www.karinaverlag.at**

Manolo Link has also published:

Ein neues Leben auf dem Jakobsweg,
and *Maria Milena.*

For more see: www.manololink.com

Printed in Great Britain
by Amazon

45010032R00111